THE DANGER
OF
MONOCULTURALISM
IN THE XXI CENTURY

Sunday Adelaja
&
Yaroslav Shumovskyi

THE DANGER OF MONOCULTURALISM
IN THE XXI CENTURY

©2017

ISBN 978-9661592604

This books is translated to English language so that it will address the problem of monoculturalism in any nation of the world. Sometimes, because of the desire for seclusiveness, nations tend to promote nationalism.

Cover Design by Olexandr Bondaruk

THE DANGER OF MONOCULTURALISM
IN THE XXI CENTURY
Milton Keynes, UK:
Golden Pen Limited, 2017

TABLE OF CONTENTS

PREFACE

The danger of monoculturalism is a book I wrote as a gift to the country of my sojourn in the last 25 years, to the Ukrainian people. At the same time, it is my hope that this book will not just benefit Ukraine in helping them build a better society, but all other peoples who will come to live in Ukraine.

This books is translated to English language so that it will address the problem of monoculturalism in any nation of the world. Sometimes, because of the desire for seclusiveness, nations tend to promote nationalism. This often leads to the isolation of other people groups from that society. The truth though is that we are all made from one and the same God. If we all come from one source, we cannot afford to distance ourselves from other humans who don't quite look like us or speak the same language as we do.

Yes, God is a God of diversity, yet God does not celebrate our diversity at the expense of other people. To celebrate your own uniqueness equals self-confidence. But to put down the uniqueness of others equals arrogance. As we celebrate our own national and cultural uniqueness, we cannot deny that other people are also unique in their own ways.

It is my hope that this book will enrich countries and nations of the earth. It is only one of the 50 books I am releasing as part of my 50th birthday celebration. Another book which emphasises the diversity of peoples and individuals is also in the list of the 50 books, it is called "the law of difference"

As I mark my 50th birthday celebration, on the 28th of May 2017, I look forward to moving back to Africa believing that this book will contribute immensely to make our world a better place for all peoples.

For the Love of God, Church and Nation.

Dr. Sunday Adelaja.

Introduction

Dear reader, this book is a cry of my soul regarding the future fate of the world at large! It addresses an issue that is affecting our modern societies globally. We understand and relate to this book clearly because it deals with what we see on the daily news, what we hear on the social media, and what is happening around the world. We need to take concrete steps to change our thinking process and start looking at things from a different point of view. Otherwise, there is a tendency for politics and media to incite hatred and intolerance towards different groups of people. Thus, leading to the repetition of past historical tragedies.

The DANGER OF MONOCULTURALISM begins with hostility and aggression towards a certain group of people. This hatred is not satisfied by eliminating that specific group from the society. Rather, it becomes a widespread prejudice and hatred towards various groups of people.

In any society, we tend to draw closer to people of the same race and nationality. As the saying goes «Birds of a feather flock together». Similarly, we can always see people from the same country in a foreign land, wanting to associate themselves with each other and create a monocultural society. For instance, the Nigerians want to associate with Nigerians only, the Indian with the Indians, the Ukrainian with Ukrainian, etc. When we look deeper

into any given country, we clearly see the segregation of foreigners regardless of their skin color and the desire to get rid of them. Even though we are one nation, there is a division of tribes and clans. This division of tribes causes tension amongst citizens of the same country. Furthermore, depending on where you live, people within the same tribe have different dialects that cause further separation with the belief that their tribe is better and wiser. Among these different dialects, there is a further division between the poor and the rich. The Rich always seeks to dominate and rule his fellow poor man.

Even within families, there is division and separation, as one feel he is better than the rest.

If we follow this path, we will create a society where we condemn and hate each other. The desire to segregate people that are different from us cannot be fully realized. In the 21st century we expect this kind of attitude to be dwindling, however, a negative and hostile attitude to others is increasing every day in every part of the world. There is a desire to segregate others on the basis of race, religion, and sexual orientation etc.

A monocultural Society is a monotonous society whereby only the representatives of one particular group have the privileges to basic civil rights. A monocultural society dictates that its culture is the only right and acceptable culture. Furthermore, people of other religions, ethnicities, and cultures may have the freedom to live, but their cultures have no place in the national culture. Why is it dangerous for countries such as Ukraine to retain a monocultural society?

This book is a study book that unveils past historical events and helps us to dive into the depth of the human soul allowing us to understand the perniciousness and doom of a monocultural society. Let us begin the journey!

PRACTICAL GUIDELINES ON HOW TO READ THIS BOOK

This book can change your life!

Often, while reading a book, we make a decision to practice everything that we learn in our daily life. Usually, after only a few weeks, we completely forget about our intentions. It is possible to have diverse knowledge on different subjects but fail to apply it in real life situations. The information in this book may not be necessarily new to you, on the other hand, it might be insightful and revolutionary. The goal of reading this book is not to acquire more information; the most important thing is what you will do with what you have learned.

Here are six practical ways, that will help you turn your good intentions into good actions:

1. Read this book several times

Regularly take breaks to reflect on what you are reading. Ask yourself how and when you can apply the recommendations. After a detailed study of the book, you should plan to reread it every month. This book should be your reference book.

2. Reading Aloud

Reading aloud enables you to release the power that backs up the words into your life. It is important that you don't just see the words but also hear them. The spoken word has a wave nature, and when it is spoken, it has a changing effect on all the surrounding objects and subjects. Remember, words matter. Do not despise the power of words!

3. Highlight and take notes

While reading this book, keep a pen or highlighter close by. Underline text and paragraphs that you found remarkable - this simple action will triple your ability to remember. In the margins of this book, write down your own thoughts and make notes - let this book become your workbook. Underlining makes the book much more interesting and enables you to quickly review it again in the future.

4. Reread the underlined segments

The advantage of underlining and noting is that you can quickly review the most important questions and segments of this book. For you to benefit fully from this book, you need to reread the book as often as possible. Let the segments you highlighted inspire you to improve your life. As humans, we have an amazing ability to forget. The only way to retain this information is to go back to it again and again.

5. Immediately apply the learned principles

When a person applies what he has learned, it helps him to better understand and remember the concept. Man cannot apply anything he has not learned. This means that learning is an active process. If you want to master the principles given in this book, apply them when necessary and as often as possible. If you do not practice them, then you can quickly forget everything. Only what is practiced remains in memory.

6. Give priority to what you are learning

At the end of each chapter, you will find "Golden Truths". These are key points that have been discussed throughout the chapter. After which you have questions and practical tasks to help you evaluate yourself effectively. Don't just read them, rather answer and examine yourself thoroughly. In order to get the maximum benefit from the practical tasks, I advise you to answer them within 24 hours. Otherwise, there is a high probability that you will forget to apply the learned principles in your life.

With my many years of experience working with people, I know that people usually perform such tasks for marks, but you are not at school. This is about your life. Studying and applying these principles helps you to build and improve your life. Therefore, I ask you to take the tasks seriously, because you are not doing it for the author of the book, but for you. To complete the tasks, it is advisable to find a quiet place where no one can distract or disturb you.

Be sure to reflect on the previous chapter and all the points that you have highlighted. Remember your decisions and write down your follow-up actions. Do not forget to schedule specific time frames and determine the boundaries that you will impose on yourself. This will help you to avoid procrastination on the planned steps to change your life in the long run. Find someone you can be accountable to for your decisions or a partner to work with.

Write down the date you started reading this book:

_____

Let that date be the turning point in your life!

HOW TO ANSWER THE QUESTIONS

The questions at the end of each chapter will help you analyze yourself and discover where you stand. In addition, this exercise will help you to realize and bring to your notice any prejudices, biases and inferiority complexes that you may have and not know. For this exercise to be effective you must be honest with yourself, spend time reflecting on past experiences and truly examine yourself. When you effectively do this, you will be able to identify your strengths and weaknesses and be able to work on them.

There is only one answer to each question. Opposite each question or statement, there is a point placed in the brackets. The accumulated sum of points will reveal your mindset in relation to monoculturalism. These questions are designed to change your attitude and outlook. They are by no means aimed at judging or humiliating you. After all, we all have something to work on.

CHAPTER 1. HOW WE TREAT THOSE WHO ARE DIFFERENT FROM US

CHAPTER 1.
HOW WE TREAT THOSE WHO ARE DIFFERENT FROM US

"If we were to wake up some morning and find that everyone was the same race, creed, and color, we would find some other causes for prejudice by noon".

- George Aiken, American General

The first factor that I will discuss in this book is the DANGER that exists in a monocultural society – which is, **the attitude we have towards those who are different from us.** We usually have different attitudes and perspectives when it comes to certain matters such as race, nationality, language, the accent of speech, social status, religious and political views, etc. A very crucial sign of civilization of modern society is tolerance towards those who are different. Whereas, an uncivilized society displays negative attitudes such as hostility and intolerance

Why is prejudice and hatred so dangerous in a MONOCULTURAL Society, especially when it is targeted towards a certain person or a group of people that have peculiar characteristics?

"ALL SORTS OF PEOPLE COME HERE"

Anyone that is unable to recognize and appreciate the differences in other people will begin to experience hatred and disgust. In a monocultural society, people have the desire to segregate the racially different ethnic group to maintain a monotonous society.

For example, there are people who are prejudiced towards other races and nationalities. They express this by saying "All sorts of people come to our country- they should go back home". From this statement, it is clear that these people have the desire to segregate and isolate themselves from people that are different. It starts with simply ignoring the foreigners, pretending not to see them, and refusing to acknowledge them.

Tatyana's story: "When I was 13 years old, I remember very clearly how I felt when I met a black man in Donetsk for the first time. Being from a small town, we used to shop in the nearest big city. One day after our shopping at the supermarket, we stood in line to pay for the groceries. As we queued to pay, a black man who also bought some groceries came and stood in line. Suddenly, there was an expression of shock on the faces of the people who had been waiting in line; they did not know what to do simply because he was a black man: whether to queue or whether to run away. One after another they began to disperse – till there was no one in line, except him. I was very frightened and I asked: «Mom, who is that?"

From Tanya's story, we can observe that people who grew up in a monocultural society exhibit fear, suspicion, hatred and shock when they encounter people that may appear different from them. In a monocultural society, a person that is distinctively different can easily create an awkward and tense atmosphere.

Note that this girl was not from a big city. This also means that since a large part of the population doesn't live in big cities or towns, the probability that they will come in contact with people of a different culture was practically zero. It is also important to note that she was not a child; she was a teenager. At this age, teenagers are already beginning to express their views on history, geography and current affairs. If they have no personal experience that enables them to get acquainted with the richness of other cultures. This makes it difficult for them to have sound judgment regarding others.

Subsequently, living together with people who have diverse cultural background will be a thorn in the side. A person that grew up in a monocultural society may not voice it out but has a deep-seated desire to create an environment that is homogeneous, predictable, and native. Such people desire to be surrounded only by those who are like them.

A song of Leonid Agutin attempts to revolutionize the conventional distrustful attitude of people towards others who appear different from them:

You are afraid of everything, but there is nothing terrible
here:
Just a guy, like a guy, just a little darker,
And it's more southerly, one darker,
There, where palm trees grow and bananas.
And there's nothing here, it's not a dream or delirium,
Do not be afraid, he's good, though unlike us!
Unlike you, unlike me,
Just like a passer-by is a black guy ..."

✳ ✳ ✳

DISCRIMINATION LEADS TO GENOCIDE

Let us now trace the DANGERS of intolerance in a MONOCULTURAL society by few historical events.

THE ARMENIAN GENOCIDE

The first example is the Armenian Genocide. This event occurred in the territories that were under the rule of the Ottoman Empire in 1915-1923. At first, the negative attitude that was directed towards Armenians was expressed in the disarmament of Armenian soldiers. Then, the deportation of well-educated and wealthy Armenians from the border areas began. Soon laws were passed that favored the deportation of all Armenians. As a result, mass deportation and murder of Armenians began.

Although at the end of the XIX century the population of the Ottoman Empire was ethnically diverse. But over time, laws were adopted that valued the superiority of Muslims. Since the Armenians were Christians, they were considered second-class citizens. In 1914, Turkey signed a secret treaty with Germany, which in particular, expressed the desire to create a monocultural society of the indigenous people of Turkey[1].

The unwillingness to accept and tolerate the Armenians led to a real genocide which claimed the lives of 1-1.5 million Armenians2. What a terrible destruction, the death of innocent people, simply because of the desire to create a monocultural society!

We observed that the desire to maintain a monocultural society inevitably led to segregation of those that differ. Ultimately the growing hatred resulted in the massacre of minority groups. This is exemplified in the Armenian genocide.

APARTHEID

The second example is apartheid. This was an attempt to create a monocultural society in the Republic of South Africa. The policy of apartheid lasted 45 years. Initially, the aim of the apartheid was to maintain white dominance by causing racial separation. At the official level, the ruling party implemented the "Race Laws" for the black and white population. During the introduction of this system, black

South Africans were deprived of almost all civil rights. Laws were passed that forbade mixed marriages and introduced a racial classification (White, Black or Coloured). It was so ridiculous that the classification into these categories was based on appearance, social acceptance, and descent. In order to be considered a white person, it took more than just a white skin. "A person could not be considered white if one of his or her parents were non-white. The determination that a person was obviously white would take into account his habits, education, speech, deportment and demeanor».

In 1950, the Land Acts separated citizens geographically on the basis of race. In 1953, a law was adopted on separate services including beaches, public transport, hospitals, schools, and universities. In the 1960s, 70s and early 80s, the government carried out forced relocations. About 3.5 million people were evicted from their homes. To oppose apartheid, the African National Congress (ANC) was created, which advocated the development of a democratic state that does not allow racial discrimination. In the early 90s, the country was on the verge of a full-scale civil war.

Let's look at the cruelty of the white people towards blacks, in the Sharpeville massacre. Between 1945 and 1952 laws were issued that forced every black man to carry a special passbook. Without permission, blacks could not look for work in the urban areas, and for the already employed, the employer had to renew this pass on a monthly basis. This pass-book should be presented at the request of any police officer. The refusal to present this document led to imprisonment. In 1960, the government extended the law of passes to women.

Early morning of March 21st, around 5,000 to 7,000 black people took part in a peaceful protest in the village of Sharpeville and asked the police to arrest them for not carrying their pass-book.

This demonstration was dispersed by the police with the help of tear gas and police batons. Then the villagers heard the news that during the day someone from the police department would make a statement about the Pass Laws. As a result, many of those who participated in the demonstration the day before began to flock to the police station in anticipation of a statement. The crowd was continuously growing in number, and significant part of it was women and children. At 10 o'clock in the morning, a squadron of airplanes flew over the assembled crowd in an attempt to intimidate the people and force them to disperse. A few hours later, the police detained three leaders of the protesters. The peaceful protesters became agitated and approached the fence surrounding the police station and suddenly shooting began.

Due to this incidence whereby 69 people, including 8 women and 10 children were killed and among 180 people wounded were 31 women and 19 children. The police forces opened fire on the already frightened crowd and most of the people were shot from behind as they fled for safety. Everything happened within 40 seconds, during which the police shot 705 bullets.

Black South Africans were brought to such a terrible state that on 25th of July 1993, four black men walked into a "white church" and killed 12 and injured 47 people. Due to the pressure from the international community, the first democratic election was conducted in South Africa and ANC party won. On May 9th, 1994, Nelson Mandela who had been imprisoned for 27 years for opposing apartheid was elected the first black president of the country.

From this historical event, we observed the growing intolerance and hostility the white South African had towards the blacks. The white South Africans had a desire to create a monocultural society which led to the segregation and the killings of black South African. The statistics reveal that in South Africa the number of murders per 100 000 population has declined from 66.9% in 1994-95 to 39.5% in 2005-2006.

Positive changes soon followed after Nelson Mandela implemented certain policies. After he won the election, he did not seek to create a similar monocultural society consisting of black people. Instead, his words clearly communicated that he understood the danger of the monoculturalism:

"During my lifetime, I have dedicated myself to this struggle of the African people. **I have fought against white domination and I have fought against black domination.** *I have cherished the ideal of a democratic and free society in which all persons live together in harmony and with equal opportunities. It is an ideal which I hope to live for and to see realized. But if needs be my lord, it is an ideal for which I am ready to die"*

KU KLUX KLAN

The third example is the Ku Klux Klan. After the end of the Civil War in the United States (1861-1865), this organization was established. It adhered to the idea of superiority of the white race and used terrorism, both physical assault, and murder, against groups or individuals whom they opposed. The Civil war which led to the death of a great number of US citizen led to the abolition of slavery. However, a significant number of white Americans

were not ready to stop being a society of only white people. This is evident in the number of people who were members of the Ku Klux Klan. Let's look at the assessments of the University of Tuskegee regarding the data on the activities of this organization:

Periods	Years	Number of Followers	Number of people killed
1st Period	1865-1870	550 000	1500-2000
2nd Period	1915-1944	3-6 million	Hundreds of people
3rd Period	Since 1946	5000-8000	Dozens of people

From this data, we observe the DANGER of intolerance, which was conveyed by the large numbers of Americans that were involved in this racist organization. Moreover, a large number of innocent people were killed simply because they belonged to a different race. This racist group was so violent that they began to kill even white Americans that worked and lived with Africans. Since the 1920s, the Ku Klux Klan has begun to persecute people on other grounds such as religion and politics etc.

This is proof that intolerance inherent in a monocultural society has a sign of barbarism. We find that the above-mentioned historical examples have been recognized by the international community as a crime against humanity.

THE GENOCIDE IN RWANDA

The fourth example is the Rwanda Genocide. This was a genocidal mass slaughter of Tutsi in Rwanda by members of the Hutu majority government. An estimated more than 800,000 Rwandans were killed during the 100-day period from April 7th to mid-July 1994. The rate of killing was five times higher than the rate of killing in the German death camps during the Second World War. Let us examine carefully what happened in Rwanda.

In Rwanda, there were two predominant ethnic groups: Hutu (85% of the population) and Tutsi (14% of the population). Although historically, their arrival on the territory of the country occurred at different periods, over time they began to use the same language hence anthropological differences were erased. Although the majority of Rwandans are Hutus, the Tutsi minority have long dominated the country. In 1959, the Hutus overthrew the Tutsi monarchy in an attempt to take control of the country and as a result clashes and killings began. The first three Tutsi leaders were removed in mid-1959 on charges of inciting violence. Further changes in the country's administration took place, such as the replacement of Tutsi officials with Hutu representatives. This led to mass riots accompanied by gun violence. By the end of the 1980s, about 480,000 Rwandans were refugees. A group of Tutsi refugees in Uganda supported by some Hutus formed a rebel group called the Rwandan Patriotic Front (RPF), which invaded Rwanda in October 1990. RPF had several

hundred members but soon grew to 7,000 and by the year 1994 there were up to 14,000 members.

At the end of October 1994, the violence of the RPF was stopped by government armed forces. With the intervention of Belgium, a truce was agreed upon, which lasted until early December. Then the war began again. Until July 1991, the war was under control, but in the space of 12 months, there was an escalation of hostility and foreign armed forces withdrew. On April 1994, an airplane carrying the presidents of Rwanda and Burundi was shot down and this led to the deaths of both presidents.

It is believed that the subsequent mass genocide was the result of hatred incited through the media: The Hutu extremists set up radio stations and newspapers broadcasting hate propaganda and urged people to «weed out the cockroaches» meaning "kill the Tutsis". People were convinced that they were involved in a good cause by killing their own neighbors[4, 5].

In this historical example, we see the terrible consequences of the seemingly harmless attitude of superiority of one group over the other.

THE TRAGEDY OF GLOBAL INTOLERANCE

The most vivid example of the embodiment of insatiable hatred for a different group of people was in Germany. Adolf Hitler was obsessed with the idea of the superiority of the "pure" German race and had the desire to provide this race with enough space to expand. Now let us trace the DANGER OF MONOCULTURLISM in this historical tragedy called the «Holocaust.»

The first group of people who experienced hatred and hostility was the Jews. In 1935, the "Nürnberg Laws» were introduced to determine whether someone belonged to the German or Jewish race. Under the Nurnberg Laws, Jews became a continuous target for stigmatization and persecution. The initial emergence of global intolerance was slowly rising. The Germans began to identify and segregate the Jews from the society. From that moment on, the Jews were forbidden to marry the Germans. Gradually, they were deprived of political and social rights, even up to the loss of citizenship.

"The aftermath of intolerance in a MONOCULTURAL society is the segregation and alienation of people who are different. In order to achieve this goal, the Nazi Government implemented a policy called the "Final Solution to the Jews Question». there was a Nazi plan for the extermination of the Jews during World War II.

This policy implied the mass destruction of the Jewish population in the whole of Europe. In one death camp called Auschwitz about 1.1 million Jews were killed. In fact, an attempt was made to completely exterminate the entire Jews population. About 4-6 million Jews (60% of Jews in Europe and about a third of the Jewish population of the world) were killed according to various estimates

What happened next? Intolerance did not end with the desire to exterminate the Jews only, but also directed towards Gypsies. From March 1936, the Nurnberg Laws that previously applied to the Jews exclusively, became applicable to the Gypsies. They were also prohibited from marrying Germans, participating in elections and their citizenship as Germans were also revoked. According to the Nazi racial theory, they were perceived as a threat to the racial purity of the Germans.

Let's note that intolerance in a MONOCULTURAL society is the breeding ground for hatred and discrimination. Pay attention to the following absurdity: an official propaganda claimed that Germans are the representatives of the pure Aryan race who came from the north and invaded India. The Aryan Race was believed to be the origin of a superior type of humanity. However, the problem for the theorists of Nazism was that the Gypsies are much more direct immigrants from India. They even speak the language of the Indo-Aryan group; hence, the Gypsies are no less Aryan than the Germans themselves. In conclusion, the DANGER Of MONOCULTURISM which is hatred towards different groups of people is devoid of logic, fact, and truth.

The arrests of German gypsies began in the early spring of 1943. Even gypsies, who served in the German army and including those who had military awards, were imprisoned. According to recent studies, the victims of the Romani genocide (Gypsies) is about 150,000-200,000.[7]

The desire to build a monocultural society was expressed in the *"General Plan of the East"*. This was the Nazi German government's plan for the genocide and ethnic cleansing on a vast scale and the colonization of Central and Eastern Europe by Germans.

The purpose of this plan was to forcefully evict the Slavic people from the territory of Poland and the occupied regions of the USSR and resettle them to Western Siberia.[8] In accordance with this plan, about 65% of Ukrainians and 75% of Belarusians were to be resettled to Siberia and the 25% «were to be Germanized». As for the Czechs, 50% were subject to eviction, and the other 50% to Germanization[9.] As we can see, even the representatives of Western Europe were not suitable for the monotonous society that was being created.

With the set agenda of creating a monocultural society, part of the "Great plan of the Nazi" was to "Germanize» foreign nationals in Central and Eastern Europe such as the Lithuanians, Estonians, and Latvians. According to

Erhard Wetzel, these particular Europeans were needed to help in managing the vast territories in the East. These Baltic people were selected for this role because they were brought up in the European spirit and «at least mastered the basic concepts of European culture.»

Furthermore, the hatred and intolerance were not only directed to non-Germans but it also affected German citizens who had African parents. They faced sterilization and persecution. The number of these victims ranged from 400 to 3 000 people[10]

We continue to observe and learn that the DANGER OF MONOCULTURISM has no end; it is an on-going violence and hatred for others. The Nazi shifted focus from other nationalities and started attacking Germans that had physical disabilities.

The T-4 killer program is the official name of German National Socialists program for sterilization, and later for the killing of people with mental disorders, retardation and inherited diseases. Subsequently, people with disabilities, as well as those who were ill for more than 5 years were amongst those being killed. At first, only children up to three years old were killed, then all age groups were included. The number of disabled people killed by 1945 exceeded 200 thousand people. In addition, from 1942 to 1945, about one million patients were tortured by hunger in German psychiatric hospitals. From 1934 to 1945, people suffering from dementia, schizophrenia, affective disorders, epilepsy, hereditary deafness and blindness, Huntington's chorea, severe deformities and severe alcoholism were forcefully sterilized. It is estimated that the number of these people ranged from 200,000 to half a million people.[11]

Again, the violence and hatred did not stop here. They began to arrest and kill men of unconventional sexual orientation (homosexuals). It is estimated that 9000 men were exterminated.[12]

Religious beliefs and practice were seen to be unacceptable and intolerable in the German Society. This led to the execution of about 2000 Jehovah's Witnesses.

Initially, you might have thought that Germany had a widespread prejudice and hatred towards various groups, but this was not so. In Daniel Goldhagen doctoral thesis titled "**Hitler's Willing Executioners,**» argues that the main reason behind the Holocaust was first **Anti-Semitism**- a hostile attitude toward Jews. Soon that hostile attitude and hatred spread like wildfire. A similar opinion is held by one of the leading experts on the Holocaust, Yehuda Bauer. Therefore, this scientifically confirms the DANGER OF MONOCULTURE. It's basically the "snowball effect" it starts from an initial state of small significance and builds upon itself, becoming larger, more serious and eventually becomes potentially disastrous.

Perhaps someone may think that it was only Hitler and the German leadership of that time that were well resolved in achieving a monocultural society. Several researchers were puzzled and wanted to know why most German citizens were actively in support of this ideology. If we do not track and analyze these tragic historical events to discover what were the root causes and their outcomes. Then, even we ourselves might plunge into this whirlpool of hatred, discrimination, and segregation of people to form a monocultural society.

Another historical book, the Bible, warned three times about the danger of monocultures, namely an increase in cross-cultural, inter-ethnic wars and conflicts over time. (Matthew 24: 7, Mark 13: 8, Luke 21:10):

"For nation shall rise against nation, and kingdom against kingdom: and there shall be earthquakes in diverse places, and there shall be famines and troubles: these are the beginnings of sorrows".

SEGREGATION OF THE LESS FORTUNATE

Now, I would like to discuss the problem of segregation that exists at different levels in Ukraine. For example, how orphans and the disabled are treated.

Doctor of Political Sciences, T.Semigina notes that the main form of social work in Ukraine with the less fortunate involves placing them in specialized residence institutions. As in the times of Soviet Union, these people are placed in closed institutions: they are not in contact with the society and the society is not in contact with them[13]. This is acceptable and a norm in many societies, as they have no desire to associate with the less fortunate and they find it easier to avoid them.

In the early twentieth century, a phenomenon called «hospitalism» was discovered in these types of institutions. This is when; patients confined in these institutions having no interaction with the outside world began to exhibit a decline in social interactions, loss of work skills and the worsening of diseases. Therefore, it was suggested to create a versatile environment, where patients would have normal daily activities and contact with others[14].

In Ukraine, the mentally disabled are unwanted in the society, for this reason, they are hospitalized on a long-term basis. This is a direct manifestation of the desire to create a monoculture. In contrast, in the mid-twentieth century, developed countries of Western Europe and the US changed their approach in their social work. They created a system whereby individuals with physical and mental disabilities were integrated into their communities. The main concerns of the citizens of these countries were how to create comfortable conditions for different people with special needs[15, 16].

MULTICULTURALISM– THE IDEAL SOCIETY

In multicultural societies, such as the United States, Canada, Australia, Singapore etc. there are policies aimed at preserving and developing cultural differences. In such societies, the rights of ethnic and cultural groups are recognized. For example, they have rights, to conduct educational activities, create and implement their own programs in the field of education, build educational institutions and open religious facilities. People see the advantages in the parallel existence of different cultures for enrichment and further development.

If you have this kind of positive attitude and approach a person of another race, you can discover and learn the good traits that exist in this race and furthermore get to know the individual as well. People of different races tend to have varying strengthens due to the different environments they come from. You should appreciate the presence of these kinds of people because you can learn and acquire a lot of knowledge and wisdom from them. When you do discover these qualities and strengths, adapt them into your life, your family and your sphere of your influence. This way you will be enriched by these virtues and it will accelerate your personal development. This should also make you realize that isolating and segregating such people limits you and significantly stagnates your growth.

However, even if you are discontent with other cultures due to certain aspects of their lives, behavior and activities there is an appropriate manner in which to express your opposition. You can do this effectively and with courtesy by logically debating ideas and creating healthy platforms for candid discussions. Your discontent should not result in hatred and absolute intolerance of the people and culture.

A vivid example of multiculturalism is in a country that is recognized as a place of harmonic coexistence of diverse groups - the Republic of Singapore. It is common to find the Chinese, the Malaysian, the Hindu and the European happily eating lunch together on the same table. On the legislative level, the government monitors the uniform dispersal of representatives of various ethnic groups in residential areas. Apartments are sold evenly to representatives of all races, so that there is no concentration of one group in a specific area, ensuring that a monocultural community does not develop. The leaders of this country perfectly understand the increasing danger monoculturalism, both from their history and from the experience of other countries.

So in this chapter, I showed you the DANGERS IN THE MONOCULTURAL SOCIETY such as hatred, hostility, and segregation of people who are different and the vicious cycle that never ends. I believe that you are convinced of the actuality of my statements based on the historical examples we discussed. In conclusion, I demonstrated a model of a civilized society, which is the "multicultural" society. In the next chapter, I will discuss stereotypical thinking that is prevalent in a monocultural society.

GOLDEN TRUTH

• A monotonous society in which only one particular group is found or enjoys basic civil rights is called a monocultural society.

• A very crucial sign of civilization of modern society is tolerance towards those who are different.

• Intolerance produces the desire to segregate people who appear different from the society.

• A person that grew up in a monocultural society may have a deep-seated desire to create an environment that is homogeneous, predictable, and native.

• Attempts to create a monocultural society is recognized by the international community as a crime against humanity

• Hatred of different people supersedes logic and obvious facts and truth.

• Let's note that intolerance in a MONOCULTURAL society is the breeding ground for hatred and discrimination.

•In multicultural societies, there are policies aimed at preserving and developing cultural differences.

•People see the advantages in the parallel existence of different cultures for enrichment and further development.

SELF-EVALUATION TEST

1. In what society did you grow up?

A) In a homogeneous society, where there were mainly representatives of my national and cultural group (1)

B) Among a society where several different ethnic groups were present but were similar to each other (2)

C) In a multicultural society, where there was a constant opportunity for joint study, work, housing with representatives of completely different races, nations, cultures (3).

2. Who do you think were more likely to carry out the crimes committed during Holocaust and other genocidal regimes?

A) Only people who were mentally disturbed (1)

B) Representatives of radical groups (2)

C) Anyone that is intolerant to other races (3)

3. Assess the personal qualities of people who are representatives of your group (race, nationality, culture, class).

A) Representatives of my group are clearly distinguished from others, we outshine all others (1)

B) Representatives of my group have obvious advantages, although in some other groups too there is something good (2)

C) I cannot assess people only by their race and nationality, each person is unique (3).

4. Identify the racial or ethnic group you perceive completely different from you and evaluate your attitude towards this group.

A) I can accept them as close relatives through marriage (3)

B) I can accept them as a personal friend (2)

C) I can accept them as neighbors living on my street (1)

D) I can accept them as colleagues in the same profession (0)

E) I can accept them as citizens of my country (-1)

F) I can accept them as tourists in my country (-2)

G) Would prefer not to see them in my country (-3).

RESULTS:

Less than 6 points. Unfortunately, the level of your tolerance for different people is extremely low. It is very difficult for you to tolerate people who do not belong to your group. Therefore, the book you hold in your hands is extremely relevant to you. You have made the right move by deciding to read it!

7-10 points. Not bad. You have an average level of tolerance. Nevertheless, this means that the potential for developing intolerance and even hatred for different people still exists. Therefore, it is necessary to carefully study this book in order to understand all the dangers of monoculturalism.

11-12 points. Excellent. Your level of tolerance is quite high. This means that you can coexist quite harmoniously with different people and groups. As you read this book you will expand your knowledge and strengthen your convictions. You can become a bearer of multicultural ideas and help other people.

RECOMMENDATIONS ON HOW TO WORK ON PRACTICAL TASKS

PLEASE NOTE: These tasks are not intended to be read-only. In order for you to make the necessary changes, you need to work through them, which is why the word «practical» appears in the title of this section of the book. Often we do this kind of exercises for marks. However, now you are doing these tasks for your own personal development. Therefore, I ask you to take the tasks seriously, because you are not doing it for the author of the book, but for you.

To get the maximum result from these tasks, it is recommended to:

1. Perform these tasks within the first 24 hours. If you delay it is more likely that you will not accomplish the tasks.

2. Study practical tasks in silence and in a calming environment. Find a quiet place where no one can disturb you: perhaps it will be a time when no one is at home or at night when everyone is asleep.

3. Make sure to reflect on the previous chapter and all the points that you have highlighted for yourself. Recall the decisions you made and write down your follow-up actions.

4. Do not forget to schedule specific time frames and determine the boundaries that you will impose on yourself. This will help you to avoid procrastination on the planned steps to change your life in a long run.

5. Find someone you can be accountable to for your decisions, or a partner to work with.

PRACTICAL TASKS

1. Give an example from your life experience when you developed a growing feeling of irritation, intolerance or hatred for a certain group of people (racial, national, cultural, social, etc.).

2. Write the reasons why you do not like this / these group/ groups of people.

3. What are the advantages and disadvantages of other groups you don't belong to?

4. What are the advantages and disadvantages of the group you belong to?

5. What do you observe in the historical examples of intolerance and genocides? What was the basis for mass bloodshed?

CHAPTER 2. STEREOTYPICAL VIEWS THAT INFLUENCE OUR ATTITUDES

CHAPTER 2.
STEREOTYPICAL VIEWS THAT INFLUENCE OUR ATTITUDES

"People are much deeper than stereotypes. That's the first place our minds go. Then you get to know them and you hear their stories, and you say, 'I'd have never guessed."

- Carson Kressley, Television Personality

In this chapter, together dear reader, we will continue our journey analyzing the characteristics of a monocultural society. In the previous chapter, I showed you the DANGERS OF THE MONOCULTURAL SOCIETY, such as hatred, hostility, and segregation of people who are different from us. Now, I want to discuss another important factor that is prevalent in a MONOCULTURAL society: which is stereotypical thinking.

A stereotype is a rigid, often simplistic representation of a specific group or category of people[17].

In a monocultural society, the development of a stereotyped and stigmatized attitude is encouraged in every possible way. What this means is; when we see a person who represents a certain group, which differs from the dominant one, we usually associate the person with a certain negative label. This happens unconsciously and without prior analysis. For instance, in our society, we can easily find people who subconsciously have a negative attitude towards black people. They believe that blacks are criminals, gangsters, bandits, or drug dealers.

Stereotypes and Prejudices in our anecdotes

There are up to 80 thousand search results on Google for anecdotes about Moldovans. All of them are Russian sites because Moldova is disregarded by Russians. Let's look at one of these jokes:

Did you hear about the Moldovan who wore two jackets when he painted the house?
The instructions on the can said: «Put on two coats.»

It is funny and it is sad! On one hand, it is humorous and people laugh, but on the other hand, it is sad because when you understand the joke, it is humiliating the whole nation of Moldovans. It is stating that they are stupid, illogical and backward.

This leads to the stigmatization of the people of this nationality. The term «stigma» was used in ancient Greece and it's a mark or a label that was put on the body ofslaves or criminals. In our time, stigma refers to a set of negative associations of a person with something shameful, disgraceful and repulsive[18].

Thus, stigmatization denotes the association of a group of people with a set of negative and often unfair beliefs. Although, these beliefs are false and groundless.

Let's take a look at another popular anecdote about gypsies. This again shows that these jokes and tales paint a negative stereotypical attitude to this nation. Pay attention to this joke:

«It's impossible to play chess with gypsies!»

- Why?

«Because they immediately steal horses!»

When we analyze this joke, it is evident that it paints a negative and stereotypical picture of Gypsies. Did you notice that it is not even talking about an encounter with a particular gypsy, rather it generalizes all gypsies? Furthermore, the joke develops a sense of superiority over other people. The reader of the joke identifies with the speaker. As a result, this makes us feel that we belong to the majority, to the group that is «good» and «does not steal horses.»

From childhood, such jokes and tales are retold and recited several times. This builds a stereotypical attitude towards the individuals of certain groups and minorities.

Jews are ridiculed on over 600 thousand Russian-speaking sites.

«Do not hit him, do not hit him!» Grandmaster is not a surname!»

In this joke, intolerance towards the Jews is really embedded. The joke that is played out here is that the Grandmaster (the highest chess rank) was confused with a Jew since Jews usually have similar surnames. But if we look deeper, we find the following sense: if he was a Jew, then he could be beaten! But this is terrible!

The number of sites that demean black people, through jokes and tales is almost one million!

What meaning do you derive from the following joke?

«There's a Negro and a Mexican in the car. Who is driving? The policeman.»

The main idea that is expressed is that black people are only capable of committing crimes and nothing else. A black man cannot be the just man that is «behind the wheel». Lawlessness, deception, theft, violence – these are the things people expect from black people in the MONOCULTURAL SOCIETY.

As you can see, it is extremely DANGEROUS to expose your mind to negative jokes and to retell anecdotes that ridicule specific nationalities or races.

How reliable are our stereotypes?

Perhaps, prior to reading this chapter, you already had stereotypical views concerning blacks, Jews, and Gypsies. Let's assess how reliable our stereotyped thoughts really are.

Suppose we believe that all black people are «gangsters», criminals, they have a propensity towards aggression and violence. Firstly, we need to examine the basis of this information, where do we get these ideas from? The source of this information is the media, TV, films etc.

What about our views concerning Gypsies? Why do we assume them to be thieves? Did someone tell us, or

did we actually have such an experience? There are always some stories that feed our prejudice. These stories are redistributed, without any concrete basis. Often, the global generalization originates from a series of identical stories that everyone simply repeats and recite.

The problem lies in the inability of people to analyze the fact that the black man they might have seen in the subway is completely separate from the black man shown on the news. Failing to recognize this causes us to condemn all black men as criminals.

We can learn from the principle in the judicial system that states the defendant is innocent until proven guilty. That is, until the judicial, law enforcement system has obvious proofs, without a shadow of doubt of the person's guilt the person cannot be blamed or charged. Our approach should also be similar in that we assume people to be innocent and not rush to pass judgment.

You could perhaps argue that people of a particular group have the same traits and characteristics, or maybe that the characteristics of an individual can be transferred to all representatives of the same group.

Then I have the next question for you. Do you realize that there are black and Gypsy people with commendable and admirable qualities and characteristics? If the idea that people of other cultures can be civilized and intelligent is unfathomable to you, we can already conclude that you are plagued with the distasteful disease of racism. The reality is that the world is full of people that are like you and me and even better, this includes both the blacks and the gypsies. If this is completely new information to you, then take the time to question the source of your ideologies.

Can we put our hand on our heart and say that black people are drug dealers? If so, then I propose the next question. How many black drug dealers do you know personally? I do not mean those whom your friends know and I do not mean the stories you have heard. Can you personally name them one by one? The answer to this question would most likely be "No". Do you see what's happening! Our society is built on speculations, presumptions, and suspicions.

I conducted a small study among Ukrainians, in which I asked them to list by name, black people they personally knew that were not drug dealers. They were able to mention at least 10 black people that are not drug traffickers. At the same time, they could not name a single black man who sells drugs. This indicates that we do not check most of our convictions and beliefs, they are not verified and they are not based on facts but on speculations.

If you personally do not know about black people, Caucasians, Chechens or gypsies who are successful, then I want to help you! Let me prove to you that our stereotypes, for example, about gypsies, are false. I encourage you to also conduct a similar study for those nationalities to which you have prejudices.

Successful Gypsies

There are plenty of Gypsies that have achieved outstanding and remarkable success. In fact, they are so numerous that this book cannot contain it, now we will look at 10 examples of such people;

Juscelino Kubitschek de Oliveira: A Brazilian statesman and politician. He was the president of Brazil in 1956-1961 and a medical doctor by profession. He is one of the most important figures of the twentieth century in the history of Brazil and one of the greatest Brazilian presidents. When he came to power, a quick jump program was initiated, and compulsory fees for foreign capital were reduced. The high-tech industry in Brazil progressed at an increased pace. In 1960, the capital was moved from Rio de Janeiro to Brasilia. This significantly increased the possibilities of developing the domestic resources of the country.

Šaban Bajramović: This person is rightly considered a legend and the musical king of Eastern European gypsies. Times magazine included him in the top ten blues performers of the world.

Nadezhda Demeter: Doctor of Historical Sciences, President of the Federal National-Cultural Autonomy of Russian Roma. A Leading Researcher at the Center for European and American Studies, IEA, RAS, OSCE and Council of Europe. An expert on Roma issues and an Author of more than 50 scientific publications, including 2 monographs.

Rosa Taikon: A Swedish gypsy, a silversmith and an active advocate of the rights of the Roma. She made a significant contribution to the culture of Sweden. Her products were displayed at more than 400 exhibitions in Sweden including in the National Museum and other prestigious galleries of the country. In 2012, Rosa Taikon received a gold medal from the Swedish government for the innovative design of jewelry. She was awarded the 2013 Olof Palme Prize for her lifelong struggle for human rights. This award acknowledged her efforts and her life demonstrated that a single individual can influence social development.

Yakov (Yang) Sergunin: Lieutenant-General, former Deputy Prime Minister of Chechnya, Doctor of Philosophy, and Candidate of Legal Sciences. He was the founder and president of the Foundation for Support of Small Peoples «Tolerance» and one of the initiators for the creation of the site «Gypsies of Russia».

Karol «Parno» Gerlinsky: A Polish gypsy sculptor, poet, and writer. He was the founder of the first elementary school for Roma children «Miri School - Romano elementaro" and a recognized public figure. His parents became victims of the Holocaust. In 2001, he was awarded a badge for achievements in the field of culture; in 2011 he was awarded the *Golden Cross Merit* for his services. His works have been repeatedly exhibited in many museums and private collections in Poland as well as abroad. His poems and stories have been translated into different languages and published in literary journals and manuals.

Johann Wilhelm «Rukeli» Trollman: A German boxer and a Gypsy by nationality. He was the light-heavyweight champion of Germany in 1933. He was killed in a concentration camp in Germany.

Mateo Maximov: A very popular gypsy author, a celebrated pastor and an evangelist. In addition to his books, Maximov is known for the full translation of the Bible into the Gypsy language (Kotlar dialect), which Gypsy Evangelists still use.

Rustam Aji: A world champion in Greco-Roman wrestling, coach of the Mariupol club «Azovmash» and Honoured Master of Sports of Ukraine. He was the coach of the national team of Ukraine for 5 years under his leadership they won 27 medals in the European and world championships.

Gyorgy Cziffra: A Hungarian gypsy that was a brilliant pianist and composer, famous for the original interpretation of classical works. At the age of nine, he entered the Academy of Franz Liszt and became the youngest student of the school. In 1950, he was arrested for political reasons. In prison, he was tortured: and knowing that He was a musician, the guards beat him on the hands and on his fingers. Furthermore, he was given selected works that caused more stress on his wrist. After his release in 1953, György had to spend a lot of effort to restore the normal operation of his hands and fingers, and in 1955 he won the Franz Liszt International Competition in Budapest. In Versailles, he organized an international pianist competition bearing his name. He created his foundation with the aim of restoring the royal chapel of Saint-Frambour in Sanlis and supporting young artists. In the Franz Liszt hall of the restored chapel, the Cziffra Foundation holds annual competitive auditions for young performers.

Looking at these examples, it is evident that gypsies also achieve outstanding results in various spheres of life such as; science, sports, music, social activities, art, politics, and military affairs.

The Danger of Stereotypical Thinking

Fred E. Jandt, a professor at the University of California in San Bernardino, author of «Introduction to Intercultural Communication,» notes that in most cases, stereotypes are not used for good purposes.

A stereotype is a thought that can be adopted about specific types of individuals or certain ways of doing things. These thoughts or beliefs may or may not accurately reflect reality. They are ready-made patterns of perception, which means that all the experiences acquired in the past determine our perception of the object at a particular moment. On the downside, the stereotype can prevent the emergence of new thoughts and ideas.

As a result of these predetermined patterns and attitudes, even when the person has new experiences and new conditions, his reaction doesn't change. This is very dangerous! For instance, you had a negative experience with a foreigner in the past. After some time you encounter other foreigners, but react to them as if it was the same situation from the past.

Stereotypical thinking makes our mind lazy, dull and quite rigid. It is easier for us to use fixed mental pictures on all representatives of the same group. We want to divide people into categories, create templates, stereotypes and a framework in which to place people in. In this way, we avoid getting to know every single person afresh each time and rather just attribute qualities that we have previously identified with his group, nationality or race. In other words, we take upon ourselves the right to deprive a person of their individuality and rather identify them with a generalized and distorted image. Our worldview then becomes oversimplified and limited we create a flawed picture of the world!

When stereotyped ideologies are debunked, it is typically confronted with hostility and aggression. An attack on stereotypes can easily be perceived as an attack on the very foundations of the universe because people raised in a monocultural society cannot acknowledge that there is a difference between the world built on stereotypes and the world in general. The DANGER then, in a monocultural society is not only the questionable sources of our judgments but also our inability to accept the truth in terms of the proven facts about other cultures.

What we basically observe in the monocultural society is the prevalence of preconceived notions and judgments. Since these judgments are groundless and made without any evidence, they are biased, harsh and inconsiderate. This type of thinking effectively inhibits us from analyzing the obvious contraindications that exist between facts and stereotypes.

Thus, our mutual understanding and how we relate to others different from us becomes more complicated. As we live in a monotonous environment, our perception of people on the basis of age, sex, race, religion, profession and nationality is distorted.

Gregory Tillett, the author of «Resolving Conflict: Practical approach», notes that prejudice towards migrants, as a rule, is based on two different stereotypes. During economic recessions, the population perceives the foreigners as invaders, who take jobs from local residents. During a flourishing economy, local residents pay attention primarily to the customs of migrants, which are contrary to local traditions. The core of both stereotypes is hatred this makes it fundamentally impossible to establish trustful and productive relations with the hated groups of the population. It is most difficult to combat stereotypes that exist in relations between two ethnic groups that have a long history of conflicts with each other.

Pascal Baudry, a professor of business administration and head of the consulting firm WDHB Consulting Group, French-born and naturalized American, published the book *"French and Americans. The Other Shore"* in which he cited a list of qualities that, in the opinion of the French, a typical resident of the United States possesses. In accordance with this list, the American is friendly and sociable, noisy, rude, intellectually underdeveloped, hard-working, extravagant, self-confident, full of prejudices, underestimating the successes of other cultures, rich, generous, incomprehensible and always somewhere in a hurry.

In turn, Harriet Rochefort, an American living in France, in the book «French Toast» wrote a list of typical stereotypes Americans have about the French. The French like the reputation of being known as the lazy people who don't speak English for ideological reasons. They are complacent, impolite and inattentive, nevertheless, they are very attentive to the ladies and art. They are guarded, so it is very difficult to get close to them. The French live in a bureaucratic socialist state and are completely dependent on officials. They do not know how to fight and the Americans had to save France twice in the 20th century. In addition, the French are filthy, they eat snails and frogs.

When France did not support the US position on the Iraqi issue, the media in both countries began to voice out old prejudices about the Americans and the French.

Similarly, negative stereotypes are present in the relations between the inhabitants of different regions of Ukraine. The danger of these negative stereotypes is that they act like a «time bomb». It's only a matter of time before this «bomb» explodes. The only way to diffuse this bomb is by developing analytical thinking.

Dissolving stereotypes by analytical thinking

In place of a superficial attitude and stereotyped thinking, we need to develop analytical thinking. This is the ability to notice details, arrange them in a logical chain and produce the desired result.

A person who does not know how to analyze what is happening around him is in great danger of being easily influenced by numerous rumors, gossips, and slanders. Moreover, the person will be misled and end up as a slave to public opinion (circumstances, etc.). Therefore, you need to consider carefully every word that you hear or read.

There are guidelines to employ in order to become an analytic thinker. These guidelines will preserve you from being deceived by the media and from being led blindly by public opinion. These simple but profound keys will also help you assess different situations and further aid in yourself examination, to check if you harbor any prejudices or stereotypes towards other nationalities.

The first point is **clarity**- when you receive any information, your first objective should be to thoroughly understand every word. One word can change the meaning of the whole sentence, article or story. If you fail to understand the meaning of even one word, the essence of what is being communicated could be lost or distorted. To ensure comprehension, find explanations, examples and other illustrations.

The second point is **reliability**- It is imperative that you verify the correctness, truthfulness and the accuracy of the information received. Determine the source of the information and confirm its dependability by finding evidence in other respected sources of information. If possible conduct your own test or research about that specific information.

The third point is **accuracy**- This involves finding all the possible data, figures, records, and statistics concerning any issue. For instance, you are told that «the percentage of Romani Drug traffickers is several times higher than the average number of most nationalities». After doing your research, you will discover that this is not so. According to the Federal Drug Control of Russia, in 2014, out of 1170 people involved in drug trafficking in Moscow, only 11 people were Romani. In 2005, 1,044 people were convicted of drug dealing, and of that number only 9 Romani people were included. It is a similar picture in other regions as well. In conclusion, the allegation that there are many more drug traffickers among the Romani in comparison to other nationalities is absolutely contrary to the truth.

The fourth point is **relevance**- When you are enquiring for certain information make sure that it is relevant and necessary. It's your responsibility to conduct an investigation. In the process of carrying out your research, it is vital that you guard your focus and pursue only what is important. Do not just be an information «garbage pit», collecting all sorts of junk information.

The fifth point is **depth**- A lot of people are proud and arrogant meanwhile they possess very shallow knowledge concerning complex and global issues. Generally, people tend to agree with a certain point of view that is similar to theirs and boldly declare it is true without thorough analysis.

Before addressing certain issues, it is needful to assess the complexity involved and anticipate challenges. For example, the issue of ending racism in the United States took centuries and was never fully resolved. Even Martin Luther King (1929 - 1968), who was an activist and a leader of civil rights movement for the black people in the United States, was killed for his desire to bring freedom to the minds of people. The issues of intolerance towards people on the basis of their differences affects all generations. Therefore, you have to understand the complexity of the issue, the intricacy of the cause-effect relationships involved, and the mutual influence of many contradictory processes that exist.

The sixth point is **Comprehension**- In the process of analyzing information, collect and compare data from different points of views. Learn about other worldview approaches to certain issues. Evaluate the information received from different sides and different participants in this issue.

The seventh point is **Logic** - Learn to come to your own conclusions. Track the logical connection between the individual words of the author. Identify the connection between a person's actions. Determine the ultimate goals and motives for what is said and done. If you lack data and you are faced with an unreasonable generalization, use your logic to draw your own conclusion.

The eighth quality is **significance** - Dear reader; your task is to identify two important key points in the information given, the meaning and the significance. Endeavor to understand the original intention of the author. That is what the author wanted you to understand and was attempting to communicate. The significance of information would then be what the information means to you and how applicable it is in your present context.

The ninth quality is **impartiality**- This is the quality of being fair, honest and just when handling any matter. First, when you are conducting a research, assess your position concerning that specific issue and examine if you have any personal interests or goals. Secondly, you have to take the place of an outside observer, the third fair-minded person. Do not take a specific side before you figure it all out. For example, are we not aware that white people also sell drugs, and not just blacks and Gypsies? So why haven't we developed such attitude towards all white people? Why don't we stigmatize all Europeans? Is it because they are white? That is not fair! The Greeks, Albanians, Ukrainians and other nationalities trade drugs as well. However, we tend to be biased in our analysis and only label a certain group. Of course, we also need to be impartial not only to the information that we have received but also in the conclusion we come to.

So, in this chapter, we have studied one important factor that exists in MONOCULTURAL society; stereotyped thinking. At first, we discussed certain racial jokes and tales people use to ridicule others and their adverse effect on our subconscious thinking. Secondly, we considered arguments that nullified our stereotypical thoughts we have towards other ethnic groups, and we used Romani people as an example. Furthermore, we established that the danger of stereotypical thinking is that, it limits our perception of the world, it deprives us of the ability to discover the truth and justice, and it sets the stage for future conflicts. In conclusion, I laid out the guidelines that you can utilize to ensure analytical thinking. This will help you eradicate shallow and narrow-mindedness. In the next chapter, we will look at another feature of monoculturalism which is classifying people by IQ.

GOLDEN TRUTH

• A stereotype is a rigid, often simplistic representation of a particular group or category of people.

• Stigmatization refers to the association of negative quality with all representatives of a certain group of people, although this relationship is absent or not proven.

• People in a monocultural society develop lazy minds, the analysis process becomes tedious for them, and the very ability to conduct an individual analysis dwindles.

• Stereotypical thinking is a way of thinking whereby we use relatively stable and simplified images of social groups, people, events or phenomena.

• In a monocultural society, a vast diversity of reality is replaced by a reduced and simplified view of it

• Stereotypical ideologies hinder us in advance from knowing the truth.

• The solution to overcoming stereotype thinking is the development of analytical thinking

• Analytical thinking - the ability to notice details, build them into a logical chain and produce the desired result

SELF–TEST TEST

1. How do you feel about jokes and tales about other nationalities?

A) Positive, I tell them myself (1)

B) Normal, I can laugh heartily (2)

C) Negative, I do not encourage such anecdotes in my environment (3).

2. Do you think that there are such national or racial groups, among whom there are no representatives superior to you in personal virtues (blacks, Gypsies, Jews, whites, Moldovans, Caucasians, Americans, Chukchi, etc.)?

A) Yes, there are groups where people cannot be as moral or smart as in my group (1)

B) If there are such people who are superior, then this is rather an exception to the rules, but in general, this group does not belong to them (2)

C) I believe that a representative from any group can potentially excel me in personal qualities: character, intelligence, abilities, morality (3).

3. On what basis do you build your ideas about different groups of people and phenomena in society?

> A) I take information from the media: TV, newspapers, discussions on the Internet (1)
>
> B) From books and from people I respect (2)
>
> C) Based on analytical thinking and research, applying the qualities discussed in this chapter (3).

4. How much do you characterize the categorization of people and communities?

> A) I try to «break up» all the categories to know what to expect (1)
>
> B) I do not aspire to have a classification of people in advance, but I notice that in some cases I am making a start in my judgments from stereotypes (2)
>
> C) I try to look at each person as an individual, regardless of his belonging to a certain group, and to recognize him directly (3).

RESULTS OF THE TEST FOR EVALUATION

Less than 8 points. We are sorry, but you have a very strong stereotypical thinking. You quite often make mistakes in your judgments and have prejudices that do not correspond to the truth. To avoid the dangers of this state of affairs, it is necessary to do a substantial work on the development of analytical thinking. This book will be a blessing to you since we will help you expand your perception of the world.

8-10 points. Not bad. You have the desire to have no prejudiced attitude towards different groups of people. Nevertheless, you do not always succeed. Part of the stereotypes that are present in your society still penetrated your mind. Therefore, your next step is to make a review of your habits in thinking, the development of a non-value attitude and the development of analytical thinking.

11-12 points. Congratulations! You worked so hard to develop the habits of analytical thinking and were able to protect yourself from absorbing common stereotypes. Stick to this approach and exert a positive influence on society by your example.

RECOMMENDATIONS ON HOW TO WORK ON PRACTICAL TASKS

PLEASE NOTE: These tasks are not intended to be read-only. In order for you to make the necessary changes, you need to work through them, which is why the word «practical» appears in the title of this section of the book. Often we do this kind of exercises for marks. However, now you are doing these tasks for your own personal development. Therefore, I ask you to take the tasks seriously, because you are not doing it for the author of the book, but for you.

To get the maximum result from these tasks, it is recommended to:

1. Perform these tasks within the first 24 hours. If you delay it is more likely that you will not accomplish the tasks.

2. Study practical tasks in silence and in a calming environment. Find a quiet place where no one can disturb you: perhaps it will be a time when no one is at home or at night when everyone is asleep.

3. Make sure to reflect on the previous chapter and all the points that you have highlighted for yourself. Recall the decisions you made and write down your follow-up actions.

4. Do not forget to schedule specific time frames and determine the boundaries that you will impose on yourself. This will help you to avoid procrastination on the planned steps to change your life in a long run.

5. Find someone you can be accountable to for your decisions, or a partner to work with.

PRACTICAL TASKS

1. Analyze an anecdote about a certain nationality. What do you see in him as a subconscious influence? What is its superficiality?

2. What is the danger of anecdotes about other nationalities?

3. Analyze the degree of competence and professionalism that those Roma's who are given in this chapter should have to achieve these heights.

4. What is the danger of stereotyped thinking?

5. Analyze the negative attitude to the group that you defined in the first chapter, in accordance with the qualities of analytical thinking.

CHAPTER 3
«THEY JUST GOT OFF THE TREE YESTERDAY»

CHAPTER 3
«THEY JUST GOT OFF THE TREE YESTERDAY»

"The less intelligent the white man is,
The more stupid he thinks the black"

- André Gide,
French author and winner
of the Nobel Prize in literature

THE DANGER of growing up in a monocultural society is that it breeds pride and arrogance; we are, therefore, unable to adequately evaluate our conditions. We are blinded to our shortcomings and are unable to appreciate the value of others. In this chapter, We will explore the division of people by intellect, social groups, classes and achievements in the monocultural society. In addition, I will discuss the common belief held by many which is the backwardness of black people and the corresponding disregard we have towards them as the less developed members of society.

I have repeatedly heard the phrase that says; "black people just got off the tree yesterday" and the idea that is put forward is that they are inferior to other people. I want to analyze all the possible interpretations and aspects of this phrase. Based on the logic of these interpretations, I will refute these arguments, and show their inconsistency!

People often do not consider the meaning of what they are saying. If we are talking about the fact that Africans physically climb trees and collect fruits, then what's wrong with that? In Ukraine people also climb trees and collect apples, cherries, apricots, etc. According to the Ministry of Agrarian Policy and Food of Ukraine, Ukrainians collect over 25 thousand tons of fruit a year! Is this degrading? This is the labor through which fruits for consumption are made available to the public.

Let's pay attention to the word *«yesterday»* in this expression. This means that the crime for which blacks are accused is not because they got off the tree, but because they got off "yesterday". Did you notice it too? This is because white people realized that they also got off the tree. But they did it earlier – and herein lies all their bravado. This small detail is simply ignored when this phrase is spoken.

After all, if the white man was also on the tree, then what is his bravado all about? The white man got off first and the black man simply followed.

For instance, if you ate a frog today, and I ate a frog yesterday how then can I mock you? In the end, we both ate a frog. If a friend of mine slept among pigs today, but it turns out I did as well just the day before, there is no room for boasting, for there is no difference between us.

It is both foolish and arrogant to perceive people to be inferior to us based on the negative situations they have been through if we too have made the same mistakes before. For instance, if I quit smoking a month ago, I have no right to scoff at those who stopped smoking a week ago. After all, I also smoked; I also succumbed to the temptation. The difference lies in the time when we overcame our challenges. But nonetheless, I want you to realize that we both faced the **same challenge** and struggled with the **same issue.** There is, therefore, no reason for boasting.

If climbing a tree is bad, then maybe it's the white people who climbed the tree first, and the black people saw and followed them. Therefore, the Europeans were the first group to set a poor example.

Let's say you have a friend that started drinking Coca-Cola as a child. You, on the other hand, preferred to drink water. Nevertheless, under the influence of your friend, you decided to follow his example. As a result, you also began to buy this drink regularly. After 5 years, your friend found out that it is better to drink juice instead for good health, and occasionally drink a cola. However, you did not immediately stop drinking coke, it took you several more years to discover this truth and change your habits. Now let's imagine that your friend condemns you for the fact that you only recently discovered what he discovered several years ago. Will this be fair? After all, it was he who first made a mistake. You just followed his example. Then what is the basis of his self-righteousness? On the contrary, one could say that it was you who followed the correct principles longer, while he had already begun negative practices for which he condemns you now.

The Peril of "white" civilization

However, the meaning most people derive from the phrase discussed above is that blacks are less developed, they just transitioned from an animalistic lifestyle and they are not civilized. People associate black people with monkeys. In fact, they insult black people by calling them "Monkey!" As an African in Ukraine, I have personally experienced this on several occasions.

Perhaps white people want this expression to indicate that they are already at a higher stage of development and progress, while others are still behind. Even if you agree with this idea, who said that these so-called «civilized» people are better off than the uncivilized blacks?

It is observed that «white» civilization comes with a much-increased risk for cancer. A large number of deadly diseases are as a result of civilization! People who still live in «primitive» cultures do not even know many of the diseases common in «civilized» countries. Doctors recently coined a new term «diseases of civilization» to indicate the main factor that causes them. The Israeli doctor, Yuri Babkin, includes heart and vascular diseases, hypertension, obesity, diabetes, cancer as well as allergies, neuroses, and osteochondrosis as «diseases of civilization».

The most common type of cancer in women is breast cancer. In a World Health Organization report, Patrick Adams points out that over the decades, the rate of breast cancer in rich countries has grown faster than in poor countries. In parts of Southeast Asia and Africa, the incidence of this disease is five times lower than in the United States. This is the lowest figure in the world! Colon cancer is found among Hindus 30 times less frequently than in the United States. Moreover, epidemiologist and cancer specialist from Oxford University, Dr. Tim Kay confirmed that when people from developing countries migrate to developed countries, then in one or two generations, they begin to have the same increased risks for diseases as those of Western countries. The issue then is the lifestyle, which is conditioned by the «blessings» of civilization.

The International Diabetes Federation has released new data on the prevalence of diabetes mellitus. The number of people with diabetes worldwide as of 2013 was 382 million people, 8.3% of the world's population. Almost half of the diabetics live in China, India and the US, and the least in Africa.

Dr. Dmitry Yu. Pushkar points out in his urology textbook, that the disease of kidney stones is the lowest amongst Africans, African Americans and Native Americans. In Europe and the United States, about 10% of the adult populations have gallstones. The number of operations carried out to remove gallstones in the world are up to 2.5 million per year. Imagine: in Moscow alone, there are up to 7000 operations per year per 100 000 population! Whereas, Africans due to their way of life are less prone to this disease!

In his book «Run for your life,» Garth Gilmore notes that countries that are proud of their high living standards, such as the United States, Australia, New Zealand, the United Kingdom and Canada, have the highest percentage of cardiovascular diseases in the world. These diseases occur much less frequently in African countries. R. Kearney and his fellow scientists also identified that the prevalence of hypertension is lower in the economically developing countries of Asia, Africa, and Latin America than in developed countries[20].

Therefore, there is no evidence that supports the notion that those who "got off the tree first" are in better conditions. On the contrary, there are obvious arguments that reflect the advantages of the way of life in Africa.

The theory of Evolution

Another argument, which is put forward as evidence of the lower mental development of blacks, is the evolutionary theory. People, who were brought up in accordance with the evolutionary theory, have the following understanding; monkeys are the least developed and the white people are the very pinnacle of development. Hence, black people fell in between these two groups. Insinuating that black people are better than monkeys, but nonetheless, they are inferior to the intellectual capacity of the white man.

At a period in time, the entire system of education of the USSR was based on the theory that people descended from monkeys, therefore it seems logical to assume that blacks are closer to monkeys. Likewise, depictions of evolution illustrate the people in the intermediary stage as dark-skinned. First a monkey, then a black race, and in the end a Caucasian race.

Beginning from kindergarten, throughout the years of school, we have been constantly exposed to this image. Hence, this picture has become embedded in our minds. The subconscious understanding of evolution is that a person becomes «whiter» as they evolve. Seemingly, the representatives of the Negroid race are closer to monkeys on the basis of these photographs. Is this really so?

Remarkably, the interpretation of this very popular image is actually quite different from its presumed meaning. The propagators of the evolutionary theory did not consider the intermediary links as Africans: for instance, the fossils of the *"Homo-erectus"* were discovered in Asia, Europe, and Africa; the fossil *"Homo Neanderthalensis"* was found in Germany; the fossil *"Homo sapiens sapiens"* was discovered in France. Therefore, even among evolutionists, these «intermediary links» are not Africans, rather European.

Furthermore, people identify blacks with monkeys, because both black people and monkeys have dark skin. On the other hand, there are also white monkeys! However, a majority of people have never seen or heard of the existence of white monkeys. If we were to consider the theory of evolution as it is understood by a large majority of people, it may well be that at the initial stage, there was a white monkey, followed by a white man, and finally the white man evolved into a black man; therefore black people are the highest pinnacle of development. This then allows me to develop the following sequence: white monkey - a white man - a black man, as a modernized result of adaptation to changing conditions. By this example, I would like to demonstrate the sheer absurdity of the analogy, which has shaped our minds regarding the association between monkeys and black people.

In fact, modern scientists do not see any substantiation in the general theory of evolution. Dr. Robert Jastrow, director of NASA's Goddard Institute for Space Studies, notes that scientists had one of two theories to choose from; either the version that life on Earth had occurred at the will of "Someone" who is beyond scientific understanding or as a result of accidental chemical reactions in an inanimate matter (the theory of evolution). George Greenstein, an astronomy professor who received his doctorate at Yale University states: "As a result of studying all the facts, unexpectedly, without any prior intention, we came across scientific evidence of the existence of the Higher Power. In accordance with the Second Law of Thermodynamics, the universe moves from the state of order to disorder. Thus, the infinitely old universe would be infinitely messy (without any life or remaining useful energy). Since there is order in the world, biological data, and usable energy, the universe cannot be infinitely old, it must have a beginning, and "Someone" had to order it". Consequently, the theory of evolution is not supported by available scientific data.

Nevertheless, let's assume that the theory of evolution was true and, accordingly, that Africans and whites, all originated from a monkey. Let's concur with the idea that white people have transitioned to the next stage of development.

It doesn't make any difference which race is akin to monkeys or which race is further ahead. It is basically like two children born of the same mother- one is older, the other younger. If we compare two siblings- the elder being 10years older, we can assume the elder has advantages in some aspects. For instance, the elder has the opportunity to explore new thing first and quickly develops a better understanding of life. In spite of the advantages the elder might have- it doesn't make him superior to the younger one. In actuality, the younger one might have even more advantages- The younger can easily learn from the mistakes of the elder, in addition, the younger can achieve greater things than the elder because the path is already set by the elder.

So now, I think, you will agree that the arguments for superiority over black people based on the fact that they "just got off the tree" don't hold up to any scrutiny. On the contrary, when we closely analyze the beliefs put forth by skeptics, we discovered that they really have no substance.

Sports vs. Intellect

I have also encountered a preconception towards black people that assumes they can only excel in sports. Thereby, implying that they are mentally incompetent, and intellectually inept. People are forced to admit that blacks are physically competent, as they win awards at the Olympic Games. However, it is said that there is minimum intelligence required to achieve success in sports. Is this true?

Looking at the world of sports, it is clear to see how it is majorly dominated by black people. They excel in every sphere of sports. Let us consider the following examples;

THE DANGER OF MONOCULTURALISM

Usain Bolt - the best in track and field athletics: six-time Olympic champion and eight-time world champion. During the Olympic Games, he set 8 world records. The current holder of world records in the race for 100 and 200 meters, as well as in the relay 4 × 100 meters.

Tiger Woods - the best in golf: 14-time winner of major tournaments putting him second place in history. Tiger received the athlete of the year Laureus World Sports Awards in 2000, 2001. In total, he won 77 PGA Tour tournaments (second place in history) and 39 European Tour tournaments (third place in history).

Michael Jordan - the best in basketball: for his phenomenal jumping ability, Michael was nicknamed «Air Jordan» and «His Airness». Jordan's individual accolades and accomplishments include five Most Valuable Player (MVP) Awards, ten All-NBA First Team designations, nine All-Defensive First Team honors, fourteen NBA All-Star Game appearances, three All-Star Game MVP Awards, ten scoring titles, three steals titles, six NBA Finals MVP Awards, and the 1988 NBA Defensive Player of the Year Award.

Pele - the best in football: the record holder for the highest number of world championships won- three titles. Participated in four world championships, the best player of the 1970 World Championship, the best young player of the 1958 World Cup, the footballer of the year in South America in 1973, twice a member of the symbolic World

Cup teams, the two-time Intercontinental Cup and the Libertadores Cup winner, the Intercontinental Champions Super Cup winner, ten time champion of the state of São Paulo, four-time winner of the Rio-Sao Paulo tournament. He is the best athlete of the XX century, according to the International Olympic Committee. Takes first place among the best players of the 20th century, according to the FIFA Football Commission, World Soccer, France Football, Guerin Sportivo (Italian sports magazine). He took first place among the best players in the history of football according to Placar (Brazilian sports magazine). Took second place in the history of the world championships, according to The Times. He is included in FIFA 100. A member of the symbolic team of the best players in all world championships by FIFA. A member of the symbolic team of the best players in the history of South America. He is one of the 100 most influential people in the world according to Time magazine.

Mike Tyson is the best in boxing: the Olympic champion among juniors in the first heavyweight division, the absolute world heavyweight champion, the champion of the WBC versions (1986-1990, 1996), the WBA (1987-1990, 1996), the IBF (1987-1990), The Ring (1988-1990). Linear Champion (1988-1990). The best boxer, regardless of the weight category (1987-1989) according to the magazine «Ring». The best athlete abroad (1987-1989) by the BBC version. He is included in the International Boxing Hall of Fame (2011), the World Boxing Hall of Fame (2010), the Nevada Boxing Hall of Fame (2013) and the wrestling hall

THE DANGER OF MONOCULTURALISM

of fame (2012). At the 49th annual WBC convention in Las Vegas, Mike Tyson was introduced in the Guinness Book of Records and in an earnest atmosphere received two certificates: for the highest number of the fastest knockouts and for becoming the youngest world heavyweight champion. He is the holder of several world records, not beaten to this day: the youngest world heavyweight champion (at the age of 20 years, 4 months and 22 days); The youngest absolute world champion in the heavyweight division (at age 21); the boxer who spent the least time from the moment of his debut to win the title of champion and the absolute world champion in heavyweight (1 year 8.5 months and 2 years 5 months respectively); The first and only absolute champion who won three major titles successively one by one; The highest paid heavyweight in history; Of the ten most expensive battles in the history of boxing, Mike Tyson took part in six; defended the title of the absolute champion (WBC, WBA, IBF) 6 times in a row; The largest number of the fastest knockouts (9 KOs in less than 1 minute); The fastest knockout at the Youth Olympic Games (8 seconds).

Winning at the Olympics and at diverse competitions means they overcame an opponent. For one does not compete with oneself, but with an opponent. Having won in varying competitions indicates that they are competent and capable.

Despite the fact that everyone admires their athletic achievements, the preconception that black people are built in terms of physique and the white man is intellectually superior still prevails. Some Ukrainians don't attend my church because it's pastored by a black man. They feel that they cannot be taught by a black man. The mindset of some individuals does not permit the idea that a black man can know more than they do.

Before I discredit the myth of the lack of successful blacks in other areas outside of sports, let us analyze the required skills and expertise that enable athletes of any nationality to succeed and thrive in sports.

Since I watch sports, I and all those who engage in professional sports, found that in order to win one needs more than just physical ability. There are a lot of tactical things involved. In sports, it is not the strongest, who wins, but the most practical and skillful. It is not the strongest football team that wins rather it is the team with the best strategy and tactics. For instance, take a boxer or a chess player – as a matter of fact, it's true amongst all athletes, it is not the strongest that wins. The best boxer is one who has tactics. He has methods and strategies. Victory depends on small things: breathing, head movement, hand, and foot coordination, it's all mental work. Probably, it is only the person who has never part taken in sports, that associates athleticism with primitivism. Primitivism is not displayed in the one who excels in sports, but rather in the one who assumes that sports are solely a display of physical capacity without the use of one's mind.

THE DANGER OF MONOCULTURALISM

Let's turn to experts in sports and sports analytics. Arkadiev Vitaliy Andreevich - Honored Master of Sports, the founder of the national school of fencing, several time champions and medalist of the championship, honored coach of the USSR, under whose leadership the men's team was world champion 8 times in a row, who trained champions of the Olympic Games and the world at large in private and team tournaments. He made the following statement:

"Tactics are present whenever two people are engaged in a combat: in war, in politics, in self-defense, in sports, etc. Tactics are specific skills; it is the ability to fight on the basis of understanding the combat situation as a whole. It requires taking into account the capabilities and aptitudes of the enemy, individual characteristics, and potential. Tactics affect the outcome of many sports and, therefore, it attracts a growing attention of coaches, athletes, and scientists. It is crucial in sports where athletes compete one-on-one, i.e. in martial arts, boxing, fencing, etc.

In track and field, the main tactic lies in causing other competitors to be disadvantaged by speeding up the pace of the race.

The tactic of a weightlifter is the ability to select attempt weights, so as to ultimately defeat the opponent. In boxing and wrestling, tactics consist of the ability of athletes to use all their energy, physical, technical and volitional capabilities in a decisive encounter with the opponent.

Therefore, it becomes obvious that if black athletes win, this is undoubtedly the result of an incredible amount of mental exertion. The winner in sport does not only have physical abilities but unique mental abilities. He has developed his mind so much that he can control the smallest details, act with the precision of a jeweler and use excellent strategies and tactics. This is not only carried out at the time of training but also in the heat of the sporting combat. The ability of man to have mastery over his physical, emotional and mental state demonstrates the complexity and intricacy of humans.

Also worth noting is requisite for a strong will and spirit. This is the result of character development; it is achieved only by continuous work on oneself. Everyone wants to relax and remain in their comfort zone, whereas athletes who win choose to work hard on themselves. These are examples of courage, heroism, perseverance, resolution and dedication. Is it possible to say then that such people are less developed and backward?

Significant invention of black scientists

So, we were convinced that even if black people achieve success only in sports, it would already be reason enough to admire them and see them as examples. I also want to expose the myth that they achieve results only in sports. Let's look at some inventions by black scientists.

Air conditioning: It was invented by Frederick Jones on July 12, 1949. This scientist, who received more than 40 patents in the field of refrigeration, developed air conditioning for military hospitals, and also invented the portable refrigerator. He also invented the automatic cooling system.

The first American clock: It was invented by Benjamin Banneker in 1753.

Automatic lighting control: It was invented by Granville Woods on January 1, 1839.

Automatic reel for fishing: It was invented by the J. Cook on May 30, 1899.

Automatic gear shift and direction indicator for cars: They were invented by Richard Spikes on December 6, 1932, and in 1906, respectively.

Baby carriage: It was invented by William Richardson on June 18, 1899.

Folding bicycle frame: It was invented by Isaac Johnson on October 10, 1899.

Biscuit cutter: It was invented by Alexander Ashbourne on November 30, 1875.

The world's first blood banks, suitable for transfusion: Invented by Charles Drew in 1945.

Gamma-electrical cell: It was invented by Henry Sampson on July 6, 1971.

Multi-functional chest of drawers with mirror: It was invented by Thomas Elkinson on January 3, 1897.

Automatic clothes drying machine: It was invented by the George Sampson on June 6, 1862.

Cornice: It was invented by S. Skreton on November 30, 1889.

Holder for the cornice: It was invented by William Grant on August 4, 1896.

Round door handle and door stopper: It was invented by Osborne Dorsey on December 10, 1878.

Dustpan: It was invented by Lawrence Ray on August 3, 1897.

A mechanical whisk for egg whites: It became the first prototype of a mixer. It was invented by Willis Johnson on February 5, 1884.

Lamp with carbon filament: It was invented by Lewis Latimer on March 21, 1882.

Elevator with automatic doors: It was invented by Alexander Miles on October 11, 1867.

Protective eye glasses: They were invented by Powell Johnson on November 2, 1880.

A metal fire escapes: It was invented the scientist Joseph Winters on May 7, 1878.

Improved fire extinguisher and automatic fire extinguishing system: It has been used in the buildings of America since 1874. Both were invented by Tom Marshall, a fireman on October 26, 1872.

A folding bed and a folding chair: They were invented by Leonard Bailey on July 18, 1899, and jointly by Brodie and Sergvard on June 11, 1889, respectively.

Fountain Pen: It was invented by the William Pervis on January 7, 1890.

Wheels for furniture: They were invented by David Fisher on March 14, 1876.

Gas mask: It was invented by Gareth Morgan in 1912.

Electret microphone: It was invented by James West in 1962. This invention is used in 90% of all currently produced microphones in the world.

Golf Tee: It was invented by George Grant on December 12, 1899.

Modern-day guitar: It was invented by Robert Flemming on March 30, 1886.

The ISA bus system and the 1 GHz RISC memory (one-gigahertz computer processor chip): Mark Dean invented the ISA bus system, which allows you to connect various devices to the computer, including printers and modems, and he is involved in creating a processor chip RISC clocked at 1 GHz in 1981.

Hair brush: It was invented by Lyda Newman on November 15, 1898.

Certifying seal: It was invented by William Pervis on February 27, 1883.

The modernized horseshoe: It was invented by James Ricks on March 30, 1885.

Ice cream scoop: It was invented by Alfred L. Cralle on February 2, 1897.

Multiple-effect evaporator: It was invented by Norbert Rillieux on December 10, 1845. This machine was used to produce premium quality sugar. This device is used to this day not only in sugar production but also in the production of glue, milk, soap and other things.

Ironing board: It was invented by Sarah Boon on December 30, 1887.

Key holder: It was invented by Frederick Loudin on January 9, 1894.

Modern day flashlight: It was invented by Michael Harvey on August 19, 1884.

Lawn mower with a rotary blade: It was invented by John Burrow on May 19, 1889.

Lawn sprinkler: It was invented by J. Lessler on May 4, 1897.

Lemon squeezer: It was invented by John Tomas White on December 8, 1893.

The door lock: this device was an improvement on the 4000-year old bolt invented by the Chinese; it became the prototype of modern door locks. It was invented by Washington Martin on July 21, 1889.

Automatic lubricator: It was invented by Elijah McCoy on November 15, 1895. It keeps engines of locomotives and ships lubricated and is still used in trains.

A lunch box It was invented by James Robinson in 1887.

A mailbox: It was invented by the Paul Downing on October 27, 1891.

A modern Mop: It was invented by Thomas Stewart on June 11, 1893.

Modernized engine: It was invented by Frederick Jones on June 27, 1939.

Modern day peanut butter: It was invented by George Washington Carver in 1896.

Pencil sharpener: It was invented by John L. Love on November 23, 1897.

Telegraphony and multiplex telegraph: They were invented by Granville Woods in 1884 and 1887 respectively.

Improvement of the player piano: It was invented by Joseph Dickinson on January 8, 1819.

The refrigerator with improved efficiency: It was invented by John Standard on June 14, 1891.

Improved riding saddle: It was invented by William Davis on October 6, 1895.

A modern rolling pin: It was invented by John Reed in 1864.

Shampoo headrest: It was invented by Charles Bailiff on October 11, 1898.

Spark plug: It was invented by Edmund Berger on February 2, 1839.

Improved hair straightener: It was invented by Madame Voker in 1905.

Street- sweeper: One of the first such machines was invented by Charles Brooks on March 17, 1890.

Three color traffic light: It was invented by Gareth Morgan on November 20, 1923.

Tricycle: One of the varieties of such a bicycle was invented by black Matthew Cherry on May 6, 1886.

3D glasses: that is used to watch movies in 3D were invented by Kenneth Dunkley in 1985.

Home security system: It was invented by Maria Van Brittan-Brown in 1968.

The Shoe-polishing machine: It was invented by Jean Matzeliger in 1883.

Laser treatment of cataract: It was invented by Patricia Bat in 1981.

The spectrograph: invented by George Carruthers, was used in space in Apollo 16 in space in 1972 to study the radiation of the ultraviolet spectrum of the Moon. In addition, the spectrograph made more than 200 photographs of the earth's atmosphere: including magnetic fields and photographs of the ionosphere.

Humidifier: It was invented by Rufus Stokes in 1968.

Space spectrometer of X-ray images: It was invented by George Alcorn in 1984.

Jenny coupler: which connects train wagons together was invented by the Andrew Beard in 1897.

It's just incredible how many beneficial and worthwhile contributions blacks have made to the world of science! Many of the things we use were invented by black scientists, a majority of whom we have never heard about before.

Classifying people by IQ

As the conclusion of this chapter, I would like to evaluate the states in which a person or a group is indeed «backward» and less advanced intellectually. Nonetheless, even if they are backward what's wrong with that? For instance, Western Europe is ahead of the countries of the former Soviet Union. We, too, are somewhat backward. I do not see the problem with being undeveloped. If we closely scrutinize the idea of «backwardness», you will quickly realize that we are all somewhat backward!

Let's carefully read the following parable:

«Once upon a time there was an elderly Chinese woman who had two large pitchers. They hung over the ends of the yoke that lay on her shoulder. One of them had a crack, while the other was impeccable and always contained a full portion of water. At the end of the long journey from the river to the house of the old woman, the pitcher with a crack always remained half filled. For two years, this happened every day: the old woman brought home only one and a half pitchers of water. The pitcher that was whole was very proud of its work, and the poor pitcher with a crack was ashamed of its insufficiency and was upset that it could do only half of what it was made for.

At the end of the two years, he was convinced of his inadequacy, so the pitcher turned to the old woman:

«I'm ashamed of my crack, which always leaks water.»

The old woman grinned: «Did you notice that there are flowers growing on your side of the path, and not on the side of the other pitcher? On your side of the path, I sowed seeds of flowers, because I knew about your crack. So every day when we go home, you water the flowers. Two years in a row, I was able to cut these wonderful flowers and decorate our table with them. If you were not what you are, then this beauty would not exist, and it would not beautify our home.»

In this story, about a pitcher with a crack, it can be seen that external differences do not determine the value of something. The pitcher, who was impeccable, was proud of his characteristics, but still did less good. Weakness can be turned into strengths. They can help you achieve certain results that a person without these weaknesses would find very difficult to achieve.

Therefore, one of the DANGERS of MONOCULTURALISM is «intellectual fascism». In general, fascism is understood as convictions based on illogical assumptions that the possession of a certain set of individual characteristics that are «supreme» in relation to other individual characteristics automatically ensures the enjoyment of political and social privileges. Intellectual

Fascism lies in the fact that people build relationships with others on the basis of their intellect. If a person is less developed, then we no longer accept the possibility that he can teach us something. In this case, we are superior to others on the basis of intellectual abilities and thereby support the idea of infringement of their rights.

Tell me, please, which of us chose our parents? Or which of us chose the country in which we were born? None of us. Hence why should we be proud? There is no merit in being born in a country where there is a developed education system or a favorable environment. If our pride is based on the idea that the whole black race «just got off the tree», then we are just proud that we were born in different family and country. This pride is absolutely groundless because we did not do anything to earn it.

So, in this chapter, we saw that the DANGER of MONOCULTURALISM includes the disregard of black people on the basis of the idea that they are less developed intellectually. First, it became obvious that what they were condemning, they themselves had done before. Secondly, we found arguments that prove that civilization has it's a downside. Thirdly, we discuss the evolution theory and came to the conclusion that even in accordance with this approach, there is no reason to assert superiority over black people. On the contrary, I cited arguments that radically change the notion of their shortcomings. Next, we analyzed the reasons for the outstanding results of black people in sports and found out that it is not only just physical capabilities, but it is intellectual and tactical abilities that allow them to be achieved.

In addition, we have studied the extraordinary outcomes they have accomplished in science and the many important discoveries black scientists have made with a worldwide reputation. In culmination, I proved that even the attitude towards really less developed people should not be that of pride and arrogance. In the next chapter, we will discuss friendship based on wealth.

GOLDEN TRUTH

• In a monocultural society, We are blinded to our shortcomings and are unable to appreciate the value of others.

• It is observed that «white» civilization comes with a much-increased risk for cancer. A large number of deadly diseases are as a result of civilization!

• In sports, it is not the strongest, who wins, but the most practical and skillful.

• Many of the things we use were invented by black scientists, a majority of whom we have never heard about before.

• If we closely scrutinize the idea of «backwardness», you will quickly realize that we are all somewhat backward!

• Intellectual Fascism lies in the fact that people build relationships with others on the basis of their intellect.

• There is no merit in being born in a country where there is a developed education system or a favorable environment. If our pride is based on the idea that the whole black race «just got off the tree», then we are just proud that we were born in different family and country.

SELF-EVALUATION TEST

1. What conclusion do you make if other groups of people are less developed?

A) Since we are more developed, we are better (1)

B) Our group was at the same level before, but we already passed this stage - that means we are better (2)

C) I cannot be arrogant because I did nothing to choose my nationality, plus the best way of life has not been confirmed(3).

2. Do you consider the technological backwardness of other nations as proof of their mental ineptness?

A) Yes, such people are mentally underdeveloped and they cannot teach us anything (1)

B) There are people from these countries that are capable, but they also come to our country to study - it means our level of intelligence is higher (2)

C) The current technological state of a country is determined by a multitude of factors, not just the mental abilities of its citizens (3).

3. Is it possible to say that a person with a lower level of intelligence has less value?

A) Yes, because he is not as smart as others (1)

B) This person is also valuable, but not as valuable as representatives of my community (2)

C) No, the value of a person is not determined by his intelligence (3).

4. How do you assess the role of black people in science?

A) They did not contribute anything to science (1)

B) They made small discoveries, but mostly in the arts (2)

C) They made many discoveries that people use in their everyday life and cannot imagine their life without it (3).

RESULTS

Less than 8 points. It's a pity, but you classify people on the basis of their intellect, class, social group and achievements. You are prone to arrogance based on your intellectual level and the development of your society. You tend to derogate technologically less developed groups and peoples. At the same time, you do not admit that people from other nations are able to teach you something. This means that you are limited to the potential of only your people. You need to revise the arguments presented in this chapter and expand your horizons.

8-10 points. Not bad. You recognize the presence of certain advantages and achievements of different people. In addition, you think that these people are also valuable and can be cooperated with. But at the same time, you are arrogant on the basis of intellectual abilities, and you do not fully understand the role of various factors that influence people. You should do an in-depth study of the merits of other cultures and countries. Further chapters of the book will greatly help you in this.

11-12 points. Congratulations! You are a bright opponent of intellectual fascism. You are characterized by adequacy in assessing your position and the merits of other people. You are open to learning new things from other groups and experiencing compassion, rather than pomposity when facing less developed people.

RECOMMENDATIONS ON HOW TO WORK ON PRACTICAL TASKS

PLEASE NOTE: These tasks are not intended to be read-only. In order for you to make the necessary changes, you need to work through them, which is why the word «practical» appears in the title of this section of the book. Often we do this kind of exercises for marks. However, now you are doing these tasks for your own personal development. Therefore, I ask you to take the tasks seriously, because you are not doing it for the author of the book, but for you.

To get the maximum result from these tasks, it is recommended to:

1. Perform these tasks within the first 24 hours. If you delay it is more likely that you will not accomplish the tasks.

2. Study practical tasks in silence and in a calming environment. Find a quiet place where no one can disturb you: perhaps it will be a time when no one is at home or at night when everyone is asleep.

3. Make sure to reflect on the previous chapter and all the points that you have highlighted for yourself. Recall the decisions you made and write down your follow-up actions.

4. Do not forget to schedule specific time frames and determine the boundaries that you will impose on yourself. This will help you to avoid procrastination on the planned steps to change your life in a long run.

5. Find someone you can be accountable to for your decisions, or a partner to work with.

PRACTICAL TASKS

1. Collect a group of people and conduct a «braggart contest» with them. In this case, you yourself must participate in it. The one who brags better will win. But it will be necessary to boast not of yourself, but of your neighbor, that is how nice and honorable it is to have the best neighbor. Look closely at the one who sits to your right. Think about the person's best qualities and greatest achievements. Do not forget that this is a contest, and the one who finds more qualities in his neighbor will win.

2. Interview what feelings the participants had when they praised others.

3. Ask how people felt when they were praised.

4. Apply this exercise in life, study the value of other people and groups in your society.

CHAPTER 4
FRIENDSHIP BASED ON WEALTH

CHAPTER 4.
FRIENDSHIP BASED ON WEALTH

People who have been brought up in a monocultural society tend to have a negative, prejudiced and arrogant attitude towards other nationalities. One of the reasons for this is the assumption that people of other nationalities are poor. This makes us understand that mono-cultural society's foster attitudes towards people on the basis of material wealth.

What is worse – poverty or abundance?

According to the encyclopedic dictionary of economics and law, poverty is defined as a state of need, a shortage of vital resources, in which basic and essential needs of the individual or family for a normal life cannot be met.

The conventional misconception is that foreigners are impoverished and underprivileged. This idea gives rise to arrogance and to the feeling of superiority. Then again, let's take a close look at the facts; Ukraine is recognized as one of the poorest countries in the world, falling into the same category as the countries of Africa. This is stated in the Credit Suisse Research Institute's Global Wealth Report in 2013. According to the report, analysts reckon that 90% of Ukrainians live below the poverty line. Most Russian live in conditions poorer than that of North Africa.

Therefore, we see that even if we grew up with the privilege of material prosperity, there are no grounds for pride, at least for Russians and Ukrainians, over Africans. In addition, poverty is an extensive issue that is prevalent in every country!

Indeed, Africa is poor and a large portion of the population in Africa is impoverished. But let's ask ourselves why are they poor, yet more content? It's clear that Africans are happier! How can a person who lives in a hut without electricity and water still be more joyous and satisfied with life?

Let's think about what we prefer in life: to have happiness and contentment, or misery and abundance.

The African who was given something small will be much more grateful and happy than the European who was given something substantial. Africans are people of high values, we can learn from them- to be grateful and rejoice in what we have. Due to their outlook on life, they are happier than many Europeans who have much material wealth.

Therefore, if a person wants to live a prosperous life, they must, first of all, determine what prosperity is to them personally. It is yet to be ascertained what is more advantageous; to be poor and happy or to be materially wealthy and miserable. There are people in the western culture who have everything they need in abundance to live a comfortable life. They are what we would call «success». However, most of these rich individuals have come to realize that having things does not translate to inner happiness, joy, and contentment.

The value of a person does not consist in what a person possesses; rather it is expressed in one's ability to be content with little. It is not about how much you have, for we can have much and still not be satisfied. How much do you need in order to be content?

Indeed Africans and other nationalities worldwide struggle with the giant called poverty. However, this is not to be perceived as a vice. In my opinion, I think of poverty as a personal challenge, it is an opportunity to show generosity and benevolence. If a person derives their sense of superiority and pride as a result of the impoverished people of Africa, it speaks of the depth of their shallowness and their backwardness. It indicates a lack of humanity, integrity, and harmony with oneself.

If I need someone worse off than myself to prove my superiority, then I have no superiority! I have nothing to show off. I am not well. I am a poor man. Yes, Africans can be financially poor. Yet, the man with such a mindset is poor in a more comprehensive meaning!

For me, the poverty of others is an opportunity to be humane. This is an occasion to reach out to the poor. This is not a chance for me to show off and be lofty. Rather, it's an opportunity to become more compassionate, to serve others, to show the highest human values. For example, Western multicultural societies are engaged in charity. They do not look at their advantages as anything to boast about. On the contrary, they see this as an opportunity to demonstrate nobility. Truly rich and prosperous Europeans, as well as Americans, use their money to exhibit their compassion.

For instance, my friend was in Portland - a city in America with a population of 600 000. Despite its small population, this city is home to 25 thousand charitable organizations. This number of organizations are greater than that of Ukraine and Russia combined. In Russia, according to the Ministry of Justice of the Russian Federation, out of 108,000 public organizations, only 1,619 were charitable organizations throughout the country[21]. In Ukraine, out of 40,000 organizations, about 15,000 organizations are charitable, according to the Ministry of Justice of Ukraine. At the same time, the Ukrainian philanthropists' forum notes that less than 2,000 of them are actually operating22. Humanity is measured not by man's wealth, but by his good nature. It demonstrates the wealth of the soul, which surpasses material wealth.

Therefore, the fact that Africa is poor is not a drawback. In actuality, we can think of this whole situation in a different light; we as the rich are wasting resources that others need- that includes food and other assets. Most times, it's not their fault that they are poor- rather we are the ones that stand guilty because of our insatiable greed.

This greed has caused us to deprive those that are weaker the opportunity to acquire wealth. Furthermore, not only are we excessive, but we are also very wasteful. According to the study of the Food and Agriculture Organization of the United Nations, one-third of all foodstuffs produced for consumption are thrown away every year. Every year, consumers in wealthy countries throw out the same amount of products (222 million tons) as produced in sub-Saharan Africa (230 million tons). In addition, the amount of wasted food reaches more than half of the annual grain harvest in the world (2.3 billion tons in 2009-2010). Per capita consumer, food waste is 95-115 kg per year in Europe and North America, while in sub-Saharan Africa and in the south and southeast Asia, the figure is 6-11 kg per year[24].

According to the data of the Ministry of Agriculture and the Office of Environmental Protection in the United States, more than 40% of all food products remain uneaten. According to experts, on average, Americans throw $ 165 billion worth of food into the trash each year[25]. In Europe, 100 million tons of food are thrown out every year. In the UK, studies have shown that households throw out about 7 million tons of food per year, although more than half of them could be eaten.

The report of the Office of Communications in Brussels states that food is sufficient for everybody, but a lot of it is used inefficiently. The impact on the environment is enormous. The amount of land needed to grow all the food that is thrown away in the world every year is the size of

Mexico (the 13th largest country in the world). The water used to irrigate vainly grown crops is sufficient for the daily needs of 9 million people[26].

Keep in mind that all of this is going on while at the same time millions of children in Africa are starving! 1 billion people are starving in the world. Hence, it is unclear who has the problem.

Due to the lack of compassion and charity, other people are starving and perishing. For that reason, when considering the problem of hunger, the main emphasis should not be placed on the poverty of those starving, but on the cruelty of people who have in abundance. All that God has entrusted to us, has been given so that we can enrich others. We need to change our attitude.

Consequently, the problem of poverty in Africa does not speak of the superiority of developed countries but of the savagery that manifests itself in an indifferent complacency.

The Law of cyclic development

When I laugh at the weak only because of their weakness and start showing off, it actually shows that I am weak.When we observe nature, we see this phenomenon at work. When a child is born, it is usually weak, then as it develops as an adult it become strong, but this strength diminishes with age. It is clear from nature that everything goes through a cyclic phase.

Scientists have long discovered the existence of a cyclical development in history. Well recognized Russian economist, N. D. Kondratiev noted that the material situation of countries is moving along spiral processes. A professor of economics Y.V. Yakovets points out the existence of cycles in economic, social, scientific, technical and environmental spheres.

Therefore, everything in the world is changing. Meaning sooner or later Africa will be the richest continent!

In the Global Innovation Index (GII-2014), compiled since 2007, the international business school INSEAD distinguished countries in sub-Saharan Africa because no region of the world has made such a breakthrough as these states. The increase in export in the countries south of the Sahara (Black Africa) inspires hope in the hearts of Africans – they too can expect a future similar to the rise of the "Asian tigers" in the second half of the XX century. Major business has changed their focus from the minerals of the Black Continent to the rapidly growing army of African buyers and labor.

According to data received at the end of 2014, from the International Monetary Fund[28] and the World Bank[29], Nigeria's Gross Domestic Product (GDP) was in 20th place in the world! This is the data obtained from the recalculation of purchasing power parity. It is believed that this indicator accurately reflects the level of GDP because it takes into account the difference in the cost of living in diverse countries. In the list of countries for the nominal value of GDP, that is, in the price of the country, Nigeria ranks 23rd and 25th according to the International Monetary Fund[30] and 31st according to the World Bank.

It surpasses countries such as Poland, Holland, Belgium, Ukraine, Malaysia, Czech Republic, Austria, Norway, Kazakhstan, Portugal, Denmark, Belarus, Bulgaria, Latvia, Sweden, Singapore, and Switzerland.

The African Development Bank (ADB) in its latest annual report predicts that this year, foreign investment in the African continent will reach a record $ 80 billion. Moreover, most of this money will go to the production sector, and not just to extract raw materials, as previously.

Exports from the countries of Black Africa grew from 68 billion dollars in 1995 to more than 400 billion in 2012. About 300 billion were exports of minerals, but in contrast to the recent past, a significant and ever-increasing part of the growth comes from other sectors of industry. According to ADB, in 2010 the African middle class grew to 350 million people from 126 million in 1980.

According to the forecasts of global chief economist at Renaissance Capital, Charles Robertson [32] , Africa's economic growth will not only continue, but it will so increase in subsequent decades that by 2050, the GDP of the African continent will be commensurate with the GDP of the United States of America and the European Union combined! The facts gathered in the study of historical processes indicate that the development of Africa will be able to compete with the similar growth of the "Asian tigers".

Therefore, do not assume that the poverty of countries is a final verdict. The world's richest man and philanthropist, Bill Gates presented a report in 2014, in which he dispelled the idea that poor countries are doomed to remain poor. In his view, if one goes back to the facts, in the 1950s, most countries were poor, whereas now they are considered an exception to the rule. Since the 1990s, the number of people living below the poverty line has halved (now more than 1 billion people). Even Africa, which most millionaires consider the poorest and most hopeless region, is getting richer: in the last 15 years, the income level in sub-Saharan Africa has grown by two-thirds - from $ 1,300 to $ 2,200. Furthermore, for the past ten years, seven countries of the African continent regularly enter the top ten fastest growing economies. In addition, the life expectancy on the continent has increased, as well as the level of education (now more than 75% of African children complete schools against 40% in the 1970s), which indicates an improvement in the quality of life.

It is worth noting that the attitude of the native people in the countries of the former Soviet Union and Europeans towards Africans and Asians is very different. In Europe, 40% of people disregard Africans and Asians. They consider them inferior to themselves, however, they are still convinced that foreigners can become like them and even better. On the other hand, in the countries of the former USSR, 95% of people may have prejudices towards different nationalities (Caucasians, Gypsies, Africans, and Chechens) but moreover, they cannot accept the idea that foreigners can be on the same level as them, not to mention being better than them.

In multicultural countries, for instance, if a foreigner works well, he has the opportunity to improve the quality of his life. Foreigners tend to be hard workers, as a result, after moving to a new country, they will begin to lead even better lives than the locals.

Africans are not satisfied with the benefits that come with just moving to Europe, they want to achieve something more, they aspire to be the best in everything. There is a popular saying that if you are at the hospital and see an African doctor and a white doctor, then always choose the African doctor. The idea being communicated is that if an African has learned something, he will be the best at it.

Thus, the poverty of individuals is also not a final verdict. I urge us to change our attitudes towards poor people! Those who needed food yesterday will feed us tomorrow.

Let's look at some concrete facts.

Oprah Winfrey lived with her grandmother for six years and wore dresses made of sackcloth. Now the wealth of this African- American woman, according to Forbes, is estimated at $ 2.7 billion.

The family of Sam Walton lived on a farm in Oklahoma during the Great Depression. In order to make ends meet, he helped his family milk cows and deliver milk to customers. He also delivered newspapers and the sold magazines. He later founded Wal-Mart, the world's largest retail chain, which ranked high in the rating of Global Powers of Retailing 2013.

In the early 90's, J.K. Rowling was a divorcee living on welfare with a child. She wrote most of "Harry Potter" in a cafe. "Harry Potter" became popular and brought success to Rowling, whose wealth is now estimated at $ 1 billion.

Ingvar Kamprad was born in a small village in Sweden and established a business that eventually became IKEA, the world's largest sales network for the sale of furniture and household goods.

Sheldon Adelson grew up in a wealthy district of Massachusetts, where he shared a room with his parents and three brothers. His father was a Lithuanian and worked as a taxi driver, and his mother owned a store of knitted goods. At the age of 12 he started selling newspapers, and a few years later he ran a vending machine for sale. Now he is chairman of the board and executive director of the corporation Las Vegas Sands. According to data for 2014, his fortune is estimated at $ 38 billion.

Del Vecchio was the son of a widow, one of five children. He went to work at a factory for the production of molds for auto parts and spectacle frames, where he lost part of his finger. At the age of 23, he opened his first store, which later grew to the world's largest manufacturer of solar and medical glasses. Luxottica produces brands Ray-Ban and Oakley, the company has 6 thousand retail outlets, Del Vecchio's state is estimated at $ 11.5 billion.

Li Ka-Shing's family fled from mainland China to Hong Kong in 1940, Li Ka-Shing's father died of tuberculosis. Li Ka-Shing was only 15 years old. He dropped out of school and started working at a plastics plant to help the family. By 1950, he was able to open his own company, Cheung Kong Industries. Initially, he was engaged in the production of plastic, and then changed the profile of activity to real estate. He then increased his stake in various companies, and today he owns shares in different companies: banks, mobile phones, satellite television, cement production, retail stores, hotels, transportation, airports, electric power, steel-making, ports, etc. In 2012, he was the richest man in Hong Kong and Asia, and also ranked ninth among the richest people in the world (according to Forbes magazine, Li Ka-Shing's capital was $ 25.5 billion).

Aliko Dangote. This Nigerian started his business by borrowing money from his uncle and opened a tiny firm at the age of 21. This firm has grown so big that it's engaged in cement, sugar and flour production. He became the richest man in Africa with a fortune of about $ 20 billion, and in 2014 Forbes gave him the 23rd place in the ranking of the richest people in the world.

Black-American Ursula Burns grew up in the apartment building on the Lower East Side of Manhattan, and now runs Xerox, one of the world's leading printing and document management companies, a pioneer in the mass production of copiers.

From the stories of theses people, it can be concluded that one cannot despise the days of small beginnings. The key value of a person is not in their current material wealth, but in their character and ability to learn and improve their life.

Reflecting on African History

Imagine the state of people when they are under the rule of a dictator: People do not have freedom and are forced to do only what is beneficial to the dictator. We clearly understand that such dictatorial structure is the cause of a delay of development, violation of human rights and poverty of people in a country. Similar patterns are observed in colonized countires[33].

Africa is not only under the rule of dictators but has also experienced colonization. According to the group of authors of the study "The Impact of Colonization on the Economic Development of Africa" from the University of Tennessee[34]. The goal of colonization was the exploitation of physical, human and economic resources in favor of the colonizing country. The expansion of colonization and the division of Africa by European states stopped the natural development of the African economic system. The Atlantic slave trade existed in Africa for more than 300 years! The demand for African slaves stimulated its development.

One of the consequences of colonization, according to the scientists at the University of Tennessee, was the subordination of the African economy to the interests of Europe. In particular, the colonialist turned Africa into a source of raw materials, they used these raw materials to produce goods for consumption in Europe. Production, which would ensure a stable national economy, did not develop, and on the contrary, it was done away with. It was precisely this that led to the gap between the development of Europe and Africa [35]. This bias in the economy is still in effect until this day.

The economic goals of colonization were to provide maximum economic benefit to the colonialists at the lowest possible cost. As a result, even independent African countries that were developing economically became subordinated to the European economic policies. For the key colonialists - the British, the French and the Germans - the immediate needs of the colonies were not important. Europe at that time was rapidly developing and decided to meet its needs at the expense of the natural resources of Africa. The quality of production in Africa did not improve. The fate of its economy depended entirely on European demand.

As noted by the English academician, professor and researcher Roland Oliver [36], the development of education in Africa was considered unimportant, unnecessary and was carried out only on a private level.

Africa has become an unequal partner in international trade. The development of local infrastructure was neglected, except for important transportation links used for exporting goods. Furthermore, the West is still using "Black labor" because they know that they have no education.

Therefore, if we have previously looked down on Africans, then let us now analyze: who is more to blame - the one who was enslaved or the one who enslaves? Of course, he who enslaves! Imagine that armed robbers came to you, took everything that belongs to you and locked you up in the cellar for 25 years. Who is to blame - the one who was locked up or the armed robbers? This example reflects what Europe has done. Often we consider Africans to be poor without taking their history into account. It is necessary to examine the factors that led to this poverty.

Consequences of classifying by financial status?

We can focus our attention on the fact that the majority of the people in Africa lives in poverty and are judged based on how they dress. And are looked down on. Is it really how a person dress that determines their essence? Many people in Europe and the former soviet union judge Africans based on their outward appearances. If we do this, we will build a society that is materialistic. We start classifying people based on their possession thinking that the rich are better.

The professor of the university of Hawaii, R. Rummel notes that the division of society by wealth can lead to hostility. This hostility can escalate to war, as the gap between the classes increases. We can see these examples in the Russian and French revolution.

Our world upholds one of these two values: (1) external values such as wealth, property or (2) Internal values such as character. The Western and European society has a materialistic outlook on life. Their focus is primarily on material wealth, things such as houses, apartments, cars, etc. Whereas, Africa still retains its core values such character, generosity, and nobility. The way a person is dressed is irrelevant because he can still be kind, brave, and healthy.

Western civilization believes that the value of a person is in their possession. As a result, people become proud on the basis of what they have. However, most Africans, whom we consider primitive, are humble. Even when they greet each other, they communicate respect through their posture. They have more respect for other people; they are more cordial and hospitable. They have more qualities that everyone would like to have, but it is more difficult to develop these qualities: such as humility, respect, and honor. These are the kind of qualities that God values - internal qualities. What does it lead to when we assume that the main values are material things? When we focus on material things above internal qualities, it usually leads to wars, such as world war 1 and 2.

As Thomas Hobbes, the English philosopher, the founder of the theory of social contract and the theory of state sovereignty, stated: «We find in human nature three main causes of war: (1) rivalry; (2) distrust; (3) A thirst for glory." In these words, it is very clear that wars arise because of the desire to acquire more external, material resources. Material values were the object of competition. In addition, Hobbes notes the cause of wars to be a lack of internal virtues and a lack of interpersonal values. And, finally, in his studies, it is evident that it is the universal orientation toward external and material features, the desire for fame, the hunger to excel externally that motivates people in enmity with each other.

The Europeans, in spite of the fact that they were mostly Christians, made a slave trade out of people. They thought that since Africans looked inferior and poor, that they could kill them and take possession of their land. They came to enslave and seize their resources. The Africans expressed their perplexity by saying: "We did not come to you, we did not attack you, we received you as guests, we even gave you some of our women - why did you repay us like this, that you took us as slaves"?

The Russians often say that it was the Europeans who were responsible for such acts, and they take pride in the fact that they did not participate in colonization. On the other hand, the Russians had serfdom. This is even worse - they made slaves out of their own people. At least, the colonialists "had enough conscience" to enslave others. Whereas, serfdom is also considered as slavery. Thus, Konstantin Aksakov, a literary critic, historian and linguist, wrote in an address to Emperor Alexander II in 1855: "A yoke was placed on the land, and the Russian land became as it were conquered ..., The Russian monarch became

A. Herzen, Russian publicist, writer and philosopher referred to the Russian serfs as "White slaves". Likewise, the chief of the corps of gendarmes, Count Alexander Konstantinovich Benckendorff, in a secret report addressed to Emperor Nicholas I, acknowledged: "In all of Russia, the only victorious nation, the Russian peasants, are in a state of slavery; All the rest: Finns, Tatars, Estonians, Latvians, Mordvins, Chuvashes, etc. - are free".

Where is savagery? Is it the African who is poorly dressed on the outside, yet fully clothed on the inside? Or is it the representatives of monocultural society who can be dressed externally to cover up internal nudity. Children in European societies are brought up in families that emphasize on how to dress well, sit well, speak well, everything is focused on the outside, designed to impress others.

Whereas, in Africa, parents have a profound understanding of life. They teach their children to think beyond what to wear and what to buy. Even amongst the most primitive peoples, the elders say: "leave the house and go into the forest for a year or two, develop your spirit, study the laws of the soul and improve your internal qualities". In modern day Africa-family, children are taught to honor, respect and helps others.

That's why, when I see a person, I don't judge him based on his outward appearance. I ask questions such as, What drives him? What are his core values? What are the principles he lives by? How does he view the world? These things are more important to me than his material possession.

I own two houses and they are considered the biggest houses in the region of Kiev. However, I do not think that I should boast of the fact that I have something that others do not have. I believe that this property has been entrusted to me. I have not forgotten where I came from and because of this, I have not become proud, nor arrogant. This brings me to draw the conclusion that, I have to help others - because I could be in their place, I recognize that all I am today is not by my own power but because God entrusted these things to me. I must serve with what has been committed to me because I can lose it. I see no reason to disregard other people or races by thinking that they are inferior on the basis of material wealth.

So, in this chapter, we talked about the danger of building relationships on the basis of material wealth. You were convinced that the danger of monoculturalism is that people become so engrossed with their own lives and ignore the needs of others. I showed you that the poverty of other people gives us the opportunity to become more humane. We also saw that we should not be puffed up by the fact that we are stronger or better at something because everything in life changes: both in the case of African countries and individuals, we saw that the last can become the first.

We made an excursus into history and discovered the role of the colonialists in the poverty of certain regions. Thus, we came to the conclusion that we cannot superficially judge by the material condition of people, but it is necessary to take into account the context. Finally, I contrasted the two existing systems of values in the world and showed that the danger of monoculturalism is that a world-view based on the pursuit of material wealth leads to enmity, wars, and bloodshed. Shielding yourself from other nations is isolating yourself from the advantages of other cultures. In the next chapter, we will understand the danger of constructing judgments based on the appearance of a person.

GOLDEN TRUTH

• Ukraine is recognized as one of the poorest countries in the world, falling into the same category as the countries of Africa.

• The African who was given something small will be much more grateful and happy than the European who was given something substantial

• If I need someone worse off than myself to prove my superiority, then I have no superiority!

• The poverty of other people gives us the opportunity to become more humane.

• All that God has entrusted to us has been given so that we can enrich others.

• When we observe nature, we see this phenomenon at work. When a child is born, it is usually weak, then as it develops as an adult it become strong, but this strength diminishes with age.

• Do not assume that the poverty of countries is a final verdict

• Often we consider Africans to be poor without taking their history into account. It is necessary to examine the factors that led to this poverty.

• We cannot superficially judge by the material condition of people, but it is necessary to take into account the context.

• Our world upholds one of these two values: (1) external values such as wealth, property or (2) Internal values such as character.

• Shielding yourself from other nations is isolating yourself from the advantages of other cultures.

SELF- EVALUATION TEST

1. What did your parents and the environment in which you grew up focus on?

A) The main thing is to look good in the eyes of other people, to behave in such a manner as to please everyone (1)

B) To gain a status in the society through education, family status, financial success (2)

C) Development of character, life values , and principles, spiritual development (3).

2. Why does God entrust a person with great success?

A) So that the individual can show-off and prove he is better than others (1)

B) For enjoyment (2)

C) To be a blessing to those that do not have, to share and enrich others (3).

3. What is your first reaction when you get an extra amount of money?

A) Think about what I can buy for myself, what I have been dreaming of for a long time (1)

B) Allocate money for the blessing of loved ones, parents and those that helped me reach this stage in life (2)

C) Allocate money for charity, look to help those in need (3).

4. What do you do when you see the poverty and need of other people?

A) I think that I deserve the good things that I have because I'm better (1)

B) I am grateful that I am not in this situation (2)

C) I think this is my chance to show humanity and help others with what I have (3)

RESULTS

Less than 8 points. Unfortunately, you are characterized by a system of values focused on the external and material. You are inclined to be proud of your position and your achievements. Your desire is to spend all you have on yourself. When confronted with a group of people seemingly poorer than you, you perceive them as inferior.

You need to thoroughly study what this attitude can lead to, and how detrimental it can be to the society at large.

8-10 points. Not bad. You take responsibility for your life and purposefully strive to move ahead. You are pleased to look good in the eyes of other people and your loved ones. Because of this, the financial status of your family is important to you. However, you are focused on yourself and your status in society. You rejoice when you get something in life, and enjoy it. At the same time, you rarely think about charity. You do not fully understand the set of factors that determine the reasons why you were awarded certain resources. You should reconsider your role and the role of your society in relation to people in need, both within your group and in other groups.

11-12 points. Congratulations! Your value system is built on inner values and virtues. Therefore, you do not evaluate people by their material. At the same time, you strive to develop, and when you achieve results, acquire new benefits, you are looking for the opportunity to share this with others. You do not focus solely on your family, but pay attention to other groups in your community. You adequately assess the nature and purpose of wealth. Use your wisdom to help more people, and pass this value system to other people within your society.

RECOMMENDATIONS ON HOW TO WORK ON PRACTICAL TASKS

PLEASE NOTE: These tasks are not intended to be read-only. In order for you to make the necessary changes, you need to work through them, which is why the word «practical» appears in the title of this section of the book. Often we do this kind of exercises for marks. However, now you are doing these tasks for your own personal development. Therefore, I ask you to take the tasks seriously, because you are not doing it for the author of the book, but for you.

To get the maximum result from these tasks, it is recommended to:

1. Perform these tasks within the first 24 hours. If you delay it is more likely that you will not accomplish the tasks.

2. Study practical tasks in silence and in a calming environment. Find a quiet place where no one can disturb you: perhaps it will be a time when no one is at home or at night when everyone is asleep.

3. Make sure to reflect on the previous chapter and all the points that you have highlighted for yourself. Recall the decisions you made and write down your follow-up actions.

4. Do not forget to schedule specific time frames and determine the boundaries that you will impose on yourself. This will help you to avoid procrastination on the planned steps to change your life in a long run.

5. Find someone you can be accountable to for your decisions, or a partner to work with.

PRACTICAL TASKS

1. What is the result of a system of values and views aimed at external and material attributes in assessing their lives, other people and peoples?

2. Nigeria is the 20th largest GDP in the world, so write at least 20 countries that it has overtaken, if the only countries to which it has given up are the United States, China, India, Japan, Germany, Russia, Brazil, France, Indonesia, Great Britain, Mexico, Italy, the Republic of Korea, Saudi Arabia, Canada, Spain, Turkey, Iran and Australia.

3. What is the purpose of the benefits that I receive in my life?

4. What is the principle of cyclical development? Give an example from your life or acquaintances when you saw its manifestation.

CHAPTER 5. JUDGING OTHERS BASED ON PHYSICAL ATTRIBUTES

CHAPTER 5.
JUDGING OTHERS BASED ON PHYSICAL ATTRIBUTES

"Hating people because of their color is wrong. And it doesn't matter which color does the hating. It's just plain wrong."

- Muhammad Ali

In this chapter, I want us to become aware of another DANGER that exists in a monocultural society which is when people are judged on the basis of their appearance. What really defines the essence of a person- is it their appearance or their inner self?

Is it accurate to judge people by the size or shape of their body? Does the body reveal the true essence of a man? As good as a having a well-built body is, does it make an individual better than others? Or can we say having a smaller body makes you better? If blacks are judged on the basis of their skin color, then why do the whites strive to sunbathe during the summer season and then show-off their tan?

Strange as it may seem, even in the 21st century, people evaluate others according to external attributes like the size and the shape of their body. Physical features such as the color of the skin, the shape of the head, nose, eyes, height, hair, are not what defines who a person is. However, people who have grown up in a monocultural society judge others by these external attributes.

This phenomenon is commonly called **racism.**

The Origin of Racism

Racists are people who believe that the innate biological characteristics of a person determine their behavior. Racists believe that national identity is determined by racial purity. According to this concept, the value of a person is determined not by his personality, but by belonging to a particular "racial population".

From a racist point of view, the answer to the question, what determines the essence of a person- is their appearance and not their true self.

The definition of racism according to human rights states- This is a social prejudice that exists in relation to a group of people, on the basis of physical characteristics (such as, skin pigmentation, typical facial features, hair texture, speech, manners and other ethnic indices) that are clearly visible, without taking into consideration other significant qualities such as intellect or talent.

The world-view of a racist is devoid of any logic. They segregate others not because of any physical handicaps or illnesses, but as a result of specific physical attributes that distinguishes them from the members of the monocultural society.

On August 28, 1963, Martin Luther King, leader of the Black Civil Rights Movement in the US, described his Dream in combating discrimination, racism, and segregation as follows: «*I have a dream that my four little children will one day live in a nation where they will not be judged by the color of their skin, but by the content of their character*».

In 1852, Count Joseph Arthur de Gobineau published his book "The Inequality of Human Races". He was supported by biologists Haeckel and Galton. These men tried to scientifically substantiate the idea of the inequality of races, but through the years, their research proved to be questionable. Therefore, it was universally recognized as groundless, unprovable and pseudoscientific.

Another theory that contributed to the development of racism is the Darwinian evolutionary theory. «**Survival of the fittest**» is a phrase that originated from this theory and served to divide humanity into "the strong" and " the weak".

Houston Stewart Chamberlain, an Englishman, migrated to Germany after marrying the daughter of the German composer Wagner. From the teachings of Gobineau and Lapouge, he developed the racist ideas which encouraged the superiority of the German race over other races. He introduced the racial theory with much aggression and also acted as a committed supporter of the struggle to preserve the "purity" of the race. Chamberlain was the first in Germany, who laid the "foundations" of the theory of races and "eugenics."

Frances Galton, the cousin of Charles Darwin, was the leader of the "eugenics" movement. Eugenics is a set of beliefs that is targeted at improving the hereditary properties of a person. The teaching was intended to combat the phenomena of decadence in the human gene pool. Just as the best representatives of the breed are selected in animal husbandry according to the proponents of these ideas it is necessary to select the best representatives of mankind. Galton used their idea to confirm that the Anglo-Saxon race was the best breed for world domination.

Friedrich Wilhelm Nietzsche had a huge influence on the development of racism through his songs "the blond beast", "the Aryan,".

It's important to acknowledge that racism does not only exist in Europe but is prevalent in several countries like Japan, US, China, India and even countries of Africa and Latin America.

Forced sterilization of people in the framework of eugenic studies was designed to prevent the reproduction of people who were considered carriers of defective genetic traits. In several of states in America, many Indians and African Americans were sterilized against their will, frequently without their knowledge, while they were in the hospital for other reasons. Particularly, African women were subjected to forced sterilization because; they were believed to be unable to control their sex life and in order to limit the growth of black families applying for social benefits. This was more popular in North Carolina was[38].

Czechoslovakia established a policy of sterilizing Romani people from 1973 onwards. The civil movement Charter 77 condemned this policy in 1977-1978 as genocide, but the practice continued even after the velvet revolution in 1989.

In Sweden, from the late 30's to the mid-50s of the 20th century, a large state program for sterilization was carried out. A total of about 60 thousand people who were considered inferior to the Nordic race were sterilized. The eugenic laws were abolished only in 1976.

According to the law of sterilization in Sweden, people with difficulty in learning, who were considered mentally or racially inferior , or those who did not match the recognized Aryan standards of the Swedish nation, were forced to be sterilized.

The 72-year-old Maria Norin related her story: "My vision began to deteriorate in my early childhood. Unfortunately, my parents could not afford to buy medicated glasses for me. At school, I couldn't see the board from my desk but was afraid to say. Eventually, I was labeled as mentally retarded and was sent to a boarding school for mentally handicapped children. At the age of seventeen, I was summoned by the school principal to sign some papers. I knew I had to sign them. The next day, I was sent to the hospital and had an operation. I was told that I will never have children."

Theories of racism were finally overthrown from the scientific world in the 19th century. However, these theories still persist in this generation because of people who want to utilize these ideas to create a monocultural society and be the ruling class.

A credible analysis of racism

The Encyclopedia Britannica states that: it is a racist belief that, racial traits have a decisive influence on the abilities, intellect, morality, behavioral characteristics and personality of an individual human being.

In the previous chapters, we already examined a number of these beliefs. I clarified that mental abilities, financial status, sporting achievements, and moral qualities do not depend on a person's nationality. We can find people from different nations and walks of life that are successful in science, sports, economics, etc. Using analytical thinking, we observed the inconsistency of prejudices that associates negative qualities to people on the basis of their nationality.

As humans, the development of our personality and success in life is not influenced only by our innate, inherited traits. Our success and how well we develop in life is greatly influenced by our perceptions, responses, and decisions during challenging times. In general, our human behaviors are as a result of social conditioning, which is determined by our interaction with others.

The Prominent French racist Georges Vacher de Lapouge tried to prove that, the head circumference of the upper class in society is less than that of the lower class. He asserted that people with round heads are mentally retarded. Contrarily, statistics show that intellectually gifted people often have a large round head and brunettes are predominant among the so-called upper class. However, modern access to International data analysis refutes all the foundations of racism. Of course, the matter is not in the form of the head, but in the personality of each individual person. The statistics simply reflect the presence of this physical feature in the people being studied, it does not account for a person's abilities.

As the doctor of biological sciences, Friedman V. points out that there is no reason to believe that there is a connection between intellect and race. The only figures that were presented to the public are the relationship

between the race and the IQ coefficient. For example, a study among US residents, according to The Bell Curve41[40], showed the following results: the average IQ of African Americans - 85, Hispanic- 89, White (European) 103, Asian (Chinese, Japanese and Korean) -106, Hebrew -113.

The first point I want to make here is that even according to statistical data, the "white" people are not at all on the front line. Secondly, scientists believe that the intelligent coefficient (IQ) does not determine the level of intelligence, but the level of socialization of an individual in a particular culture. Therefore, the indicator of the average level of IQ and the characteristic of representatives of a specific nationality has been changing significantly over the decades; the gaps in these figures are declining. This indicates that race does not determine the intelligence coefficient, but it's simply the structural and social factors that were present and are present in different countries. Citizens of every country are influenced by the availability and accessibility of education.

IQ is not related to creativity, intelligence, or ability[42]. Almost all 800 teenagers with an IQ exceeding 135 points from the 50-year study of Termen and Cox in California (1921) subsequently took a high position in society, but there were no outstanding people among them. Meanwhile, it was the best 1 percent of the total number of students studied.

In reality, this coefficient determines only 10-25% of possible success in academics and professional career[44].

IQ is an indicator of social adaptability and not of talent. So, the IQ of black Americans in the above study were lower than that of white Americans and Europeans. However, the first generation of Africans that settled in the US and Britain, had equal or higher results than the white people45! At the same time, whites living in High Mountain areas had lower IQs than the other Europeans.

The influence of social factors on IQ was also confirmed by the studies carried out on orphans. In the US, children of African descent, brought up by white adoptive parents, have a 10% higher IQ than those raised non-white. In the UK, black boarding students have higher IQs than whites!

Furthermore, African immigrants in America make up the largest percentage of people to attain higher education. This puts them ahead of Americans, Asians, and Hispanics[47].

The summary of these studies is that each person is unique. Their experiences are also unique and different. However, each person's mental development and life achievements are determined by how they respond in different situations.

Anthropologists Bogdanov AP, Niederle L., Anuchin DN, Boas F., Lushan F. Verified that the physical attributes that racists attach so much importance to, especially the head circumstances, does not correlate to the socioeconomic status, and the mental abilities of people.

The United Nations Educational Scientific and Cultural Organization (UNESCO) prepared a number of historical declarations that have helped to show the groundlessness of racial prejudice: the Declaration on Race (1950), the Declaration on Race and Racial Differences (1951) and the Proposals on Biological Aspects of Racial issue (1964). The culmination of UNESCO's activities was the Declaration on Race and Racial Prejudice adopted by the UNESCO General Conference at its 20th session in 1978. In these documents, the scientific community and prominent experts established scientific evidence that refutes racist theories.

We are all predisposed to racism

At the University of Virginia, psychologists conducted a study that showed the perception people had about other races: in this test, participants were asked to select labels for people belonging to different racial groups. This labels contained positive adjectives such as «Pleasant», «wonderful», «excellent» and negative adjectives such as «disgusting», «unpleasant», "terrible», «frightening». The participants of the test had little time to interact with each other, as a result, they chose labels that were inherent in them subconsciously - Hence, the participants of the test gave their true thoughts.

It was observed that people had a high esteem for their race in comparison to others. Even though the race to which they belonged had a low social-economic status or low standing in the society, they were still committed to their own race. People felt that the group to which they belonged was the perfect.

Scientists revealed that people's subconscious decision was different from their conscious decision. The organizers of this experiment gave this explanation: our subconscious assessments usually arise from the stereotypes which are widespread in our society. And even though we disagree with these stereotypes, they still shape our perception.

Now let's analyze the people who grew up in a monocultural society. The factor of identification is so strong in these individuals that subconsciously, they see their national, racial, social or any group they belong to as the most perfect, developed, civilized, and excellent of all. Moreover, THE DANGER OF MONOCULTURALISM lies in the reality that, the natives of a particular group tend to develop a stereotypical prejudice towards people of other groups. As a result, the monocultural society nurtures a subconscious racist!

Scientists also studied what is known as the "halo effect". When a person is attractive, people tend to focus on that particular attribute and are blind to the other features. Studies have also shown that we automatically attribute positive qualities such as talent, kindness, honesty, and

intelligence to individuals who have a pleasant appearance. In a monoculture, the sense of belonging to our society is a very important factor. Thus, if a person's appearance is consistent with our socially accepted norms, we automatically esteem them.

As a result of their research, they observed that people have special preference for others who seem pleasant or attractive to them. This influences their decisions in instances when they decide a potential electoral candidate, whom to employ as an assistant, and also in judicial decisions.

An interesting study was conducted by psychologists from the University of Pennsylvania. In the course of this study, the physical attractiveness of 74 defendants was assessed. As a result of studying the court records, it was discovered that the handsome men were given less severe sentences. It was also observed that attractive defendants had twice the chance of avoiding imprisonment compared to ugly defendants. We have already established that the sense of belonging to a particular group creates sympathy in us. So, we tend to extend this feeling of sympathy to those we identify as similar to us, this significantly influences our choices.

Our point of view regarding a person or groups of people is affected by how many times we have had contact with them in the past.

An interesting experiment that proved this point was carried out: a screen showed faces of several individuals at a very rapid pace, making them unrecognizable to the participants. It was found that the more often the face of a particular person flashed on the screen, the more the participants liked this person when they engaged in subsequent interaction. In addition to this, the words of individuals whose faces appeared on the screen more often than others seemed most convincing to the participants.

From this, we see that another great DANGER OF MONOCULTURALISM is the lack of objectivity in our judgments.

The Third Wave Experiment

During the first week of April 1967, the third wave experiment movement was created by a California high school history teacher Ron Jones. Jones, finding himself unable to explain to his students how the German population could have claimed ignorance of the "The Holocaust", decided to demonstrate it to them instead[1]

Ron Jones decided to hold students through a similar experience of creating a community with a dictatorship.

Strength through discipline

On the first day, Jones taught on the advantages of discipline and established a number of new unusual rules that concerned behavior in the classroom. In addition to this, students were to preface each remark with "Mr. Jones". He recalls in his book that the students reacted enthusiastically to the idea of uniformity and strove for it as a natural need. We can observe the behavior of these students, the same tendencies that we are studying in this book - the desire for a monocultural and monotonous society. Let's see what happened later in this experiment.

Strength through community

On the second day, entering the classroom, the teacher was amazed that the students immediately followed the rules; there was an atmosphere with a high sense of discipline. This time, the principle of community was introduced. Jones revealed the advantages of the community and he explained that community is that bond between individuals that work and struggle together, it's feeling that you are part of something beyond yourself. The students chanted their motto and experienced the power that unity gives them. The movement created within the class was named «The Third Wave». A gesture of greeting was presented, something reminiscent of the greeting of the Nazis. The students had to use it even outside the classroom and they willingly complied.

Strength through action

On the third day, Jones taught about the principle of action, he explained how discipline and community were meaningless without action. He discussed the value of assuming responsibility in the community. All the students were given a membership card, making the group exclusive. Each person was assigned a special assignment, such as designing the Third Wave banner, initiating new members and the like. Many found themselves getting involved in several roles and various tasks. Even students considered unintelligent took up roles as bodyguards of the teacher.

The experiment took on a life of its own: students from all over the school began to join the "Third wave experiment". The number increased from 30 to 43 people. They began to study better and they showed extraordinary motivation. The teacher was amazed at how many students reported about those who did not follow the rules of the movement. A number of students demanded strict adherence to rules from other students and intimidated those who did not take the experiment seriously. There were even three students that were expelled from the Third wave because they didn't agree with the principles put forth.

Dear reader, do you notice the evolving danger of such a society? This is exactly what happens in a monoculture! This aspect of actions necessary to strengthen the monotony of the society creates a platform for the oppression of people considered different. Similarly, in a monocultural society, it will only be a matter of time before concrete actions are taken against those who do not conform to the standards.

Strength through pride

On the fourth day, the teacher taught the principle of pride. He taught them that being proud means knowing that you are the best, knowing that you are superior. For many, the Third Wave became the center of existence. The real Gestapo began to work in the school. The class size increased to eighty people. On this day, the teacher realized the experiment was getting out of control. As you can evidently see, the dangers involved in monocultures can easily spin out of control.

He came up with an idea to effectively put an end to it: he informed the participants that the movement had been accepted as part of the national movement and that the next day the presidential candidate from the Third Wave would announce its existence. Everyone had to gather for this honorable event.

Strength through understanding

On the fifth day, about two hundred members of the movement gathered! The teacher started with a gesture of greeting and two hundred hands responded immediately. Then he uttered the motto of the Wave, the whole assembly joined him in a chorus. They repeated it over and over. Each time the response of the crowd grew louder. After everyone was seated, Jones turned on the television, they were all eagerly waiting to be addressed by the presidential candidate. To their shock, the screen was blank, after a few minutes of silence, the teacher announced that they were part of the experiment on fascism and that they voluntarily created a sense of superiority similar to the Germans during the Nazi period.

«You think that you are elite, that you are superior to those who are not in this room. You sold your freedom for the convenience that gives discipline and excellence. You decided to give up your own beliefs and accept the convictions of the group –without question. Perhaps, you joined in just to have some fun and thought you could quit this 'game' at any time, but look at how far you have taken this movement. More importantly, the question is how far could you go? Let me show you your future.»

On that note, he showed them a film about the history of the Third Reich. The film clearly portrayed the values of pride, arrogance, superiority and discipline that were highly esteemed in the Nazi regime. It plainly depicted the horror of the holocaust and the massacre of people considered inferior with various methods such as; gas chambers, concentration camps, burnings. The room was dead silent, the students were aghast. Everyone began to analyze what was happening as if waking from a deep sleep, and for the first time, they all began to question their "dreams".

Mr. Jones elaborated that fascism is not a foreign ideology that was practiced by an estranged group of people, but rather a trait we all carry. Through this experiment, he proved how easily we could all fall for this monstrous lie.

This experiment clearly demonstrated the danger of monoculturalism. It's a time bomb. People who isolate themselves from others who are different have potential to turn into racists. This experiment took place over five days, and instantaneously a sense of pride and superiority was triggered- this is a direct effect of belonging to a monocultural society.

Therefore, politicians, who make racial and nationalistic appeals in their speeches turn out to have a large number of supporters. After all, people are given a reason to feel proud and worthy without any effort on their part. Suppose a person is lazy and refuses to improve himself. All of a sudden he is told that he is a member of an elite race and everyone that belongs to this group of people is automatically superior to others. Therefore, the privileges of identifying with a particular group provide incentive to be a supporter of such leaders.

The division of people on an external basis has potential in itself to attract new supporters. After all, we did nothing in order to acquire external attributes - skin color, eye color, head size, shape of nose; we were simply born with these features.

It would be possible to see at least some kind of logic if the bodybuilders, athletes who had spent years working on their bodies daily, felt some sense of pride. They did the work, even over their external attributes. But this required the internal qualities of character, will, perseverance, discipline, and sacrifice.

When our parents, who belonged to a certain nationality met and decided to give life to us, we had no choice. We did not influence it in any way. In turn, our parents have done nothing to be born in a particular country, to be a member of a particular race.

This makes it crystal clear that basing relationships on appearance is utterly groundless; it is devoid of logic, rationale, and truth!

Let's look at another experiment that demonstrated a predisposition to racism as soon as a monocultural community emerges, and let's evaluate the groundlessness of this «racism» together.

The «Blue eyes – Brown eyes» Experiment

Jane Eliot was born in 1933 in the city of Riceville, Iowa. In the 1960s she worked as a third-grade school teacher. Every year she spent time with her pupil (most of her pupils were children of 8 years old) talking about racial

discrimination, trying to instill racial tolerance and open-mindedness from childhood. She understood that her initial approach was ineffective - most of her students had never met black people in their lives, so discussions about racism were of an absolutely abstract nature, and were not helpful in understanding the essence of the problem. Let's see how the unplanned behavior of children in her experiment has reflected the danger and inadequacy of judging by external attributes. In 1968, the morning after the assassination of Martin Luther King, a third-grade teacher asked the children to express their views about black people. Their responses were mainly various racial stereotypes, such as, they are all mentally retarded, or that they are not able to do any kind of work.

As you see, the education of people in a monocultural society has a number of shortcomings. It is very difficult to embrace tolerance towards people who are different if everyone in the environment is the same.

The teacher asked the children if they wanted to find out what it was like to be a «Negro» and they agreed. Eliot divided the students into two groups - children with blue eyes were placed in a privileged group, and children with dark brown eyes were placed in the oppressed caste. These two groups were not allowed to interact with one another, nor drink from the same fountain.

On the first day of the experiment, blue-eyed children were allowed to play in the new gymnasium, they got second portions for lunch, they had an extra 5 minutes for recess and they were allowed to sit at the front of the class. In addition, Eliot praised them for their diligence in class. The other group, on the contrary, was deprived of all these privileges. Elliott also provided brown fabric collars and asked the blue-eyed students to tie them around the necks of their brown-eyed peers as a method of easily identifying them as the minority group.

We can learn several elements of a monocultural society from this exercise. There is always an infringement of the rights of those who are considered different and those considered elites simply because of their external features enjoy undue privileges.

At first, on the part of the pupils belonging to the minority group, there was resistance to the idea that blue-eyed pupils were supposedly better than brown-eyed pupils. To stop the objections, Eliot used the false thesis that melanin is responsible not only for the blue color of the eyes but also gives Blue-eyed pupils intellect and learning ability.

Shortly after this explanation, the events were stunning - the blue-eyed children became arrogant, bossy and began treating their «inferiors» with contempt. They learned to find their own arguments, explaining why such a state of affairs is natural, inventing derogatory names for brown-eyed people in attempt to display their superiority. The academic performance of the «superior» group dramatically improved, they could handle tasks that they previously found challenging. In contrast, the «inferior group» began to decline in their performance, they became timid and subservient including those that were previously dominant. They could not cope with tasks that they used to find simple before.

In this short-lived experiment, we can already trace the influence of the so-called «scientific racism». Artificially developed arguments that indicate superiority in appearance are easily accepted by people. In a monoculture, a person is also inclined to accept arguments about his superiority, even if these facts contradict logic.

The next day, Jane conducted the same experiment but changed the roles of the groups. The same situation was repeated - now brown-eyed children began to taunt and mock the blue-eyed children, who in turn become subservient and timid.

At 14:30 Jane stopped the experiment - she allowed the blue-eyed children to remove the collar from their brown- eyed classmates: the children literally hugged and cried with happiness as they were reunited with their friends. The teacher reminded the children that all this was connected with the murder of King, and asked them to write an essay about what they understood from the exercise. The children's essays were published in a local newspaper and then reprinted by the Associated Press.

This exercise and multiple instances of its repetition with identical results, make it clear that people quickly get used to the role of the dominance. It is also obvious that people are drawn to the idea of superiority on the basis of their external differences. If we extrapolate this case, at least in our imagination, and play it out at the level of society, then we will understand how groundless all prejudices on the basis of race, nationality, and ethnicity are. This ideology of superiority can result in national and international tragedies.

In addition, the influence of a false thesis on melanin and eye color shows how pernicious a superficial and non-analytic attitude to information can be. So in the popular Soviet science film of 1971, «I and Others» presented an exemplary experiment, which was prepared and conducted by the assistant professor of psychological sciences Valery Mukhin. In it, students were instructed to give a psychological description of a person based on their photograph.

Do you think this is reasonable task? If you analyze the essence of the task, it's basically asking the participant to draw conclusions about who the person is, simply by how they look.

At the beginning of the experiment, the first group of participants was informed that the man in the photo was a dangerous criminal. Following this, all the participants described the man as cunning, secretive and reserved. They

claimed that he had cold eyes filled with wickedness and cruelty. He appeared to be discontent, full of contempt and unreliable.

It was also noted that his rough, awkward nose is usually not characteristic of intellectual people, but indicates the narrow-mindedness of this person. They went on to assume that he is a sadist and probably drinks a lot. As each of the participants took turns to look at the picture, they gave the same description.

The second group of participants was informed that the same man in the photo was a great scientist and was given the same task. This time, the participants described him as intelligent, gentle, good-natured and reliable. They said he had a pleasant face and probably loves children. They claimed his eyes revealed intellect, depth, and wisdom.

One of the conclusions of this documentary was that «We see what we want to see.» and I think we can all agree.

Therefore, the MONOCULTURAL society is DANGEROUS because people tend to interpret the external attributes of others to fit in with their initial misinformation concerning these people. In this case, when we see a representative of another ethnic group, we imagine and think up negative internal qualities, based only on external attributes. However, we judge these attributes through the prism of the information that was originally obtained.

Remember how many times you made mistakes in your assumptions about a person when you were convinced, that person was reliable or unpleasant, and then it turned out that you were mistaken. This is the same thing that happens in a monocultural society.

The Adverse effect of discrimination and prejudice

One of the important effects that we observed in the «Brown eyes - blue eyes» experiment is how the oppressed group began to decline in their academic performance. Similarly, racism has a negative impact on people who do not conform to the racial «standards» of a monocultural society.

This is called the Golem effect. It is a psychological phenomenon in which lower expectations placed upon individuals either by supervisors or the individual themselves lead to poorer performance by the individual. This does not mean the individual will eternally perform poorly, a person under certain conditions can break this vicious circle. Nonetheless, the overwhelming majority is exposed to this negative influence on a psychological level.

This principle is the opposite of the «Pygmalion effect», which is the phenomenon whereby higher expectations lead to an increase in performance. In an experiment that later became classical, the teachers were told that among their

pupils there were some children who were very capable and some who were completely incapable. In reality, there was no difference between the two groups, and the level of ability for all students was roughly the same. However, the expectations of the teachers for the 'capable' students was higher than for those deemed 'incapable'. As a result, a group of supposedly more capable students in anonymous testing received higher grades than a group of «less» able students. The expectations of teachers in some inexplicable manner were transferred to students and influenced their real academic success.

In the sphere of professional work, the Pygmalion effect is manifested in the fact that the expectations of managers greatly influences the results of their subordinates. So, managers who highly appreciate their subordinates and expect good results from them, get better results. In the same vein, the leaders, who consider their subordinates to be a bunch of slow-witted, lazy people, get exactly what they expect- poor results. Many researchers have proved that the expectations leaders have of their staff, tend to come true.

It is argued that both of these effects come from Viktor Vroom's expectation theory, which states, that people are able to produce much better results when they believe that they are expected to get good results. The opposite is true according to the Golem effect, people perform below par if low expectations are set by the boss, the head, the teacher, etc.

It was studied how the Japanese humanitarian aid workers stationed around the world, felt and communicated with the local organizations they counseled. The scientists noted that the more positively the volunteers were met by their local colleagues, the higher organizational indicators were noticed.

Here we see that the presence of a monocultural environment with prejudices towards other nations will create a negative psychological environment and will affect the effectiveness of people.

In addition, racism has a negative impact on the health of the discriminated person. Analysis of the results of the last 66 studies, which involved more than 18,000 blacks, led scientists to the conclusion that racism has the same consequences as psychological trauma. These symptoms include somatization (psychological disorder, expressed as physical pain), anxiety and increased sensitivity to interpersonal communication.

The more monocultural a is society, the more likely symptoms of mental disorders will manifest in the population considered different. The relationship between the experience of racism with depression and anxiety can be traced quite clearly. Researchers believe that the connection between the psychological state and racism can result in problems with physical health in the object of racial discrimination. This creates the phenomenon of the so-called «health inequality» [48].

Likewise, let's consider another danger of monoculture which is mockery. This occurrence is more commonly known as «bullying», and includes a prolonged psychological or physical abuse, harassment. Bullying at school is especially bullying pervasive.

When a student is mocked and taunted based on his external differences, it literally breaks down the identity of the victim and affects the individual for a lifetime. Proof of this was presented by a group of scientists from King's College in London under the leadership of Ryu Takizawa. The observation was conducted on children born in the same week in 1958 in England, Scotland, and Wales. The were subjected to mockery at the age of 7 and 11 years. Then assessments were made after they reached the age of 23, 33, 42, 45 and 50 years.

A detailed report on the results of this study is published in the American Journal of Psychiatry. Figures confirm that victims of frequent or constant bullying in school, are more likely to suffer from depression, nervous disorders and suicidal tendencies at adulthood. Additional, they are less successful at work, earn lower incomes and are at a higher risk of being unemployed. They often lead a lonely life with no family and friends. In other words, «childish taunts» turn into quite serious adult problems.

So, in this chapter, I demonstrated the DANGER OF MONOCULTURE in the aspect of judging others based on physical attributes. We were convinced; the only thing that can be assessed by looking at a person is only appearance and nothing more.

We studied the phenomenon of racism, examined scientific research that proved that external, biological and congenital factors do not determine the essence of a man. Having examined various sociological experiments, we saw how dangerous monocultures are because of the tendency of a person to exalt the group to which he belongs, and himself on the basis of this belonging.

In conclusion, I exposed how gravely racism affects the mental state, physical health and effectiveness of people who experience these prejudice.

In the next chapter, we will study the danger of a monocultural society, and how the disregard for other races leads to devaluation of labor and, consequently, to a halt in development.

GOLDEN TRUTH

• Racists are people who believe that the innate biological characteristics of a person determine their behavior.

• "I have a dream that my four little children will one day live in a nation where they will not be judged by the color of their skin, but by the content of their character". Martin Luther King

• Mental abilities, financial status, sporting achievements, and moral qualities do not depend on a person's nationality.

• The first generation of Africans that settled in the US and Britain, had equal or higher results than the white people.

• The monocultural society nurtures a subconscious racist.

• From this, we see that another great DANGER OF MONOCULTURALISM is the lack of objectivity in our judgments.

• There is always an infringement of the rights of those who are considered different and those considered elites simply because of their external features enjoy undue privileges.

• We did nothing in order to acquire external attributes - skin color, eye color, head size, shape of nose; we were simply born with these features.

• In a monoculture, a person is also inclined to accept arguments about his superiority, even if these facts contradict logic.

• racism has a negative impact on the health of the discriminated person.

SELF-EVALUATION TEST

1. What can be determined by the appearance of a person?

    A) Abilities (1)

    B) Psychological trait (2)

    C) Appearance (3).

2. Is there scientific evidence to support the superiority of individual races?

    A) Yes, this superiority is scientifically proven (1)

    B) It is not scientifically proven, but it is clear from the difference in the development of civilization of different peoples (2)

    C) I disagree, in fact, there is scientific and s tatistical evidence that counter the theory racism - and the difference in civilizational development is due to a combination of historical and cultural conditions (3).

3. Is it right to extol your own nation (race, nationality)?

A) Yes, because my nation surpasses the rest (1)

B) Yes, it's my nation (2)

C) No, because I did nothing to belong to my nation. I did nothing to determine in which country and family to be born (3).

4. Does the race, nationality in itself affect mental abilities, moral qualities, financial status, sporting achievements?

A) Yes, the nationality of the individual determines what a person can achieve whether and if it can, then what will a person do (1)

B) Nationality has a slight influence because people of certain nations will never be able to achieve what others achieve (2)

C) No, regardless of the nation, individuals can achieve whatever they have set their minds to (3).

RESULTS

Less than 8 points. It's a pity, but you have evident racism and a sense of superiority of your group over others. Appearance is one of the key factors by which you evaluate people. Most likely, you either cling to your belonging to the group as the sole reason for pride or have been influenced by inaccurate information. You need to reevaluate the ideas that you accepted earlier and study the research that is given in this book.

8-11 points. You don't have an extreme form of racism, but, nevertheless, you are strongly influenced by the media. You feel as though the physical appearance has an influence on the inner world of man. At times, your views are totally biased and at other times you are analytical and reasonable.

Learn the scientific and life evidence of the incompetence of racism and finally get rid of prejudice on the basis of appearance.

12 points. Congratulations! You free from racism. You are not in a hurry to evaluate a person on the basis of their external attributes or race. You give each person a chance. Therefore, people are quite comfortable around you and you can work with people of absolutely different origins. You should use your knowledge to help other people get rid of.

RECOMMENDATIONS ON HOW TO WORK ON PRACTICAL TASKS

PLEASE NOTE: These tasks are not intended to be read-only. In order for you to make the necessary changes, you need to work through them, which is why the word «practical» appears in the title of this section of the book. Often we do this kind of exercises for marks. However, now you are doing these tasks for your own personal development. Therefore, I ask you to take the tasks seriously, because you are not doing it for the author of the book, but for you.

To get the maximum result from these tasks, it is recommended to:

1. Perform these tasks within the first 24 hours. If you delay it is more likely that you will not accomplish the tasks.

2. Study practical tasks in silence and in a calming environment. Find a quiet place where no one can disturb you: perhaps it will be a time when no one is at home or at night when everyone is asleep.

3. Make sure to reflect on the previous chapter and all the points that you have highlighted for yourself. Recall the decisions you made and write down your follow-up actions.

4. Do not forget to schedule specific time frames and determine the boundaries that you will impose on yourself. This will help you to avoid procrastination on the planned steps to change your life in a long run.

5. Find someone you can be accountable to for your decisions, or a partner to work with.

PRACTICAL TASKS

1. Where did the ideology of racism originate from? Give examples of countries where the ideology of racism was active?

2. What is worse? a racist from a technologically advanced country or a benevolent person without racial prejudices from a technologically backward country?

3. What are the effects of discrimination on those being oppressed?

4. Why is there no reason for pride and exaltation of one's nation (race, nationality) and humiliation of others?

5. Collect people who differ in appearance, and carry out this exercise called «What we are like». Procedure: the members of the group are sit in a circle. You invite one of the participants to come out of the circle on the basis of any real or imaginary resemblance to yourself. For example: «Sveta, please come to me, because we have the same hair color (or we are similar in that we are inhabitants of the Earth, or we are the same height, etc.)». Sveta comes out of the circle and invites another of the participants out in the same way. The game continues until all members of the group are no longer in the circle. Make a group discussion of the conclusions after the exercise.

CHAPTER 6.
PLOW AS A NEGRO, AND LIVE AS A WHITE MAN

CHAPTER 6.
PLOW AS A NEGRO, AND LIVE AS A WHITE MAN

In the previous chapter, we dealt with all the dangers of racism that are typical in a monocultural society. In this chapter, I want us to consider the absolutely undetectable negative aspect of MONOCULTURALISM like, the devaluation of diligent and hard work which is based on false exaltation, on the basis of belonging to the titular nation.

The titular nation is the single dominant ethnic group in the state, typically after which the state was named. This concept was introduced in the late 19th century by Maurice Barres, a French novelist, journalist, and politician. According to Barres, the language and culture of the state's system of education are built on this dominant ethnic group.

So, how is the value of labor in a society connected to the future of its development, as well as with the existence of a preferential treatment to the titular nation?

Labor is not a respecter of skin color

In the 1973 Soviet movie, "Headless horseman" the expression «Work, Negro, the sun is still high!» by Cassius Calhoun became popularized. From that moment, most people consciously and subconsciously began to associate hard work with black people. Naturally, since many Post-Soviet countries were monocultural societies, this phrase was not addressed to black people because they were not actually there. Now the phrase is used in reference to anyone forced to work hard, and that is the connotation behind the word «Negro». This phrase was used and is still being used in our everyday communication amongst fellow countrymen.

Let's analyze the meaning of this phrase in a broader perspective. Firstly, the idea is laid that, it is the black people who need to work hard, and to plow. This mindset emerged from the days of slavery and colonialism. A certain specialization and the distribution of labor along racial, ethnic, and social lines can be traced before our time.

In the minds of most people, there is a conflict which is: black skin is associated with plowing, and white «European» skin - with comfort. Consequently, if we analyze our speech carefully, we will find these tendencies in our conversations: "plow as a Negro - and live like a white man", "Yesterday, I bathed with hot water like a white man «, "I will go by taxi like a white man", "I want to work like a white man, and not as a black slave".

A famous Russian satirist, writer, Mikhail Zhvanetsky said: "I get 140 rubles (3$) per concert, while Michael Jackson gets 50 thousand dollars for a concert. So who is really a Negro?" Apparently, he meant that, if race played a decisive influence on the social status and the level of a person's income, his color should have influenced his income.

Another expression that indicates the association of race and degree of work by human effort is the expression, «literary Negro». It refers to a person who knows how to write well but works for another writer. He performs the time-consuming and tedious work that the author himself does not want to do. In French and Polish language, there are similar expressions with the same reference to individuals of the Negroid race. Synonyms of this expression are «literary slave», «literary laborer».

Also, in English-speaking countries (especially in the US and Canada) there is the expression «speak in white». This expression was created when the white colonialists couldn't understand the broken English spoken by the Africans and Indians (such as pidgin, creole/ autochthonous languages). The very expression originated in the American English of the south of the USA when more educated white planters scoffed at the poorly mastered speech of their Negro slaves. Later, this expression was adopted by Canadians, and it was often heard on the streets of Montreal. The rich, English-speaking industrialists constituting the city's elite expressed their negative attitude towards the French language, the

French-Canadian culture, as well as the history of the city and people. They nicknamed them the «white Negros of America.»

So, we see that the association of race with a particular type of labor and standard of living is a common phenomenon. The desire of a specific group of people to maintain a status of superiority created the environment that contributed to the emergence and spread of this mindset.

It is beneficial to «plow like a Negro»

I would like to expatiate on the **second** aspect of the phrase «Work, Negro, the sun is still high". This communicates the idea that "working as a black person» has become synonymous with something negative, undesirable, second-class, and humiliating, but I strongly disagree with this idea!

Analyzing the first aspect of this phrase, we have seen that the diligent, and focused work that was associated with black people was portrayed as something negative. Thus, the danger of monoculturalism lies in the fact that, it develops an antagonistic attitude towards work in which, people try to avoid hard labor and want to simply take positions of dominance over others that will carry out this work.

Personally, I think that black people are in fact, plowing like slaves. Despite the weather conditions, they do the dirty work and are humiliated and enslaved. However, I do not think this is a drawback. Blacks have the ability to win in life if they will maintain a good attitude while plowing.

If you plow and work all the time, choosing not to «live like a white man» - you have a future. The one who does not work has no future - he has only the present. He thinks little of those who work hard not knowing that the one who works hard has both the present and the future! When a person plows and works hard, he becomes skillful in the affairs of life. He acquires the skills necessary to perform certain tasks and eventually becomes good at what he does. As a result, he becomes capable of solving problems. When confronted with challenging situations in the future, his ability to solve problems becomes useful. Unlike a person who refuses to plow or work.

If you are a foreigner, this slavish-plowing is advantageous.

Citizens of most countries have the tendency to be more relaxed drifting through life. Whereas, foreigners have a different mindset and this affects the way they approach their work. They take advantage of all the opportunities to improve and become better in life. They are internally motivated.

Let's see what leads to the slavish, diligent work of black people!

African immigrants in the US are becoming more educated than any ethnic group born in America, including white and Asian Americans[49-53]. Most studies state that about 43.8-49.3% of all immigrants from Africa receive a degree of higher education[54,55]. This is slightly larger than the similar percentage of Asian immigrants, significantly more than the results shown by European immigrants, and almost twice as much as white Americans born in America [56, 57]!

In the UK, the Commission on Racial Equality conducted a study that showed that, when entering British universities, immigrants from China, India, and black Africans performed better than white Englishmen. In this case, blacks above the age of 30, of African descent, have the highest educational rates than any other ethnic group in the British Isles [58, 59].

Of particular interest is, the 27-year research in the UK, which studied two generations of immigrants and native English: parents and children.

In both generations, the blacks had a higher level of results on achievements in education, wage level, and employment. Behind them were Indian and Chinese immigrants. Remarkably, the children of immigrants in the second generation surpassed the achievements of their parents on average and far exceeded their white peers in most social and economic indicators[59].

As we see, the negative attitude towards hard and strenuous work that is prevalent amongst white people leads to a decline in performance from one generation to another. Conversely, the adherent one who believes in the hard working ethics of the black man experiences continuous success and development.

Even though Africans who "plow as Negroes" have been associated with having low intellect, in actuality, Africans occupy higher positions in Western countries than white Americans and Englishmen in their native countries [60, 61]. According to a number of scientists, such positions require a higher level of intelligence and greater cognitive abilities[62-64].

Now let's take the so-called white man who lives in comfort, but does not plow. This is the lottery mentality: I want to win the lottery and live richly. Nonetheless, history and facts have proved to us that those who win the lottery, but lack financial intelligence, end up losing all their money and eventually become penniless. World statistics say that 99% of people who have won millions of dollars in the lottery become even poorer in the course of time.

I invite you to look behind the scenes of the lives of the «lucky ones» who won the lottery.

At 16, a modest girl, **Callie Rogers,** who worked as a cashier for 3.60 pounds per hour, bought a ticket to the National Lottery and won 1.9 million pounds.

Having received a lot of money, Callie became wild. She dropped out of school and spent about 15 thousand pounds a day on all kinds of parties and drugs. The last of her acquisitions were silicone breasts. Within six years, she committed two suicide attempts and overdosed on drugs several occasions. Callie was so used to spending money that even when her account was empty, she could not stop spending. Eventually, she owed the bank almost 70 thousand pounds. Today Rogers is a single mother who barely makes ends meet to feed herself and her two children.

Let's draw conclusions from this story. Before winning the lottery, Callie had not acquired the necessary skills to manage finances. She was not ready for such huge amount of money. As a result, when she won the lottery, she fell into various addictions. It ruined her health, her family, and her finances. Comfort, which was not preceded by hard work, could not improve her quality of life, nor did it give her a better life, rather it worsened her condition.

Michael Carroll, an English winner of the UK National Lottery. The ex-bin-man became known as the "Lotto lout" after scooping £9.7m when he was just 19 years old. Carroll was wearing an electronic tag when he bought a lucky dip ticket in November 2002.

Soon after winning his fortune, Carroll gave gifts to friends and family. He decided to spend his fortune living like a celebrity. He bought a chic house for 325 thousand dollars, luxurious cars, and arranged alcohol parties. After Carroll left his wife, he spent around 200 thousand dollars on prostitutes in the space of eight years. In 2006, the BBC reported that he was almost bankrupt, having spent his fortune on new homes, drugs, parties, pieces of jewelry, and cars.

As a result, he had to sell all his property to pay off his debts. Now Michael works as a scavenger and earns $ 5 an hour.

This is a very revealing story! Prior to winning the lottery, this man was jobless. We can assume he lived a slothful and irresponsible life. It was almost like he was in the desert and the sudden wealth was just a mirage, a figment of his imagination, a temporary illusion. The truth is that if we could adequately assess where we are in life currently, and persistently move toward our desired state of development in our profession and character, then we will certainly achieve success. Comfort is misleading; it can cause a person to lose focus and direction in life.

Ken Proxmire, a tool-grinding machinist, won a million dollars in the Michigan lottery. Ken used his wealth to buy the Great American Dream. He moved from Michigan to California, where he started a car business with his brothers. Several years later, his business folded, and he declared bankruptcy. His son, Rick, commented: "He was an ordinary, poor guy who suddenly became rich; he wanted to try everything at once. It was a real nightmare for three or four years", he continued. "Now we no longer have daily outrageous conversations about buying limousines or a helicopter, my father lives the simple life of a machinist".

If you study the biographies of such people, you will discover that they were not accustomed to the phrase «Plow like a Negro» because of this, they did not have the necessary financial and professional competence. The lack of self-discipline in relation to their goals is transferred to the business that they started with the money they have won. But they fail, because of lack of skills.

In 1993, Suzanne Mullins won $4.2 million in the Virginia lottery. After taxes, Mullins received 20 annual payments of $47,778.84. However, for five long years, everything changed dramatically. The Associated Press reported in 2004 that she paid more than $1 million in medical bills for an uninsured son-in-law, and then took out a loan against future payments from the People's Lottery Foundation, a company created specifically to give lottery winners money up front to be repaid when annual payments arrive. When the lottery rules changed in 2000, enabling the winners to collect their money all at once, Mullins opted to take the remainder of her prize and stopped paying her loans, the AP said. She ended up bankrupt and in court. «It's been a hard road,» her lawyer, Michael Hart, said at the time. «It's not been jet plane trips to the Bahamas.»

Don't you think that these stories seem very similar, except the differences in the names? Unfortunately, this is the reality of life. Where comfort turns into vanity, unable to improve one's life or sustain it.

Gennady Teterya, a 57-year-old resident of Ukraine, became well known for winning three jackpots in the period of two years. His first win was 1.6 million hryvnia (about $ 62,000) in the «National Lottery». He later won a jackpot of 3 million zlotys (about $ 750,000) in Poland. On his return from Poland, Teterya managed to win his third jackpot of 3.4 million hryvnias. His luck was transferred to his son, who won a Tavria car in the «Loto-Zabava» lottery.

The «lucky» Gennady Teterya owed a debt of $ 2,500,000. In 2003, he began borrowing money from his friends – collecting considerable amounts to buy new lottery tickets. When people began to demand repayment of loans, he drenched himself with acetone and set himself on fire. When the creditors realized that there was really nothing to return, they began to take everything from his apartment that was of some value. It is known that even before the first win, Gennady lived in debt, and from the first jackpot, he had owed debts.

The fact that this man was already living in debt even before his first win indicates a lack of discipline and financial knowledge.

Despite being given the opportunity to live a life of comfort and ease, he could not manage this new way of life. Reluctance to «work like a Negro», that is to work diligently deprives a person of attaining a promising future.

By analyzing the lives of these people that won lotteries, we realize that prior to winning they had none of the essential skills for a successful life- they were devoid of both financial and entrepreneurial skills. However, the person that «works like a black man" and labors to attain wealth is advantaged. Even if he loses his wealth, he simply continues to work hard, because he understands that wealth is only a means and not the end.

In other words, the person who remains focused and works diligently will eventually develop essential skills and expertise. Ultimately, this person will also acquire wealth and properties, because he has already attained the skills to create wealth. The process of developing a skill is a more esteemed goal than the goal of simply accumulating wealth.

There are plenty of people with certificates, degrees, and diplomas in various specialties such as law, botany, business and even medicine, but lack the necessary skill and practical knowledge. Personally, I would prefer having the skill rather than the certificate.

«To work like a black man» – In my opinion, is a compliment. It's the best thing that can happen. The one who lives like a white man lives in comfort. Comfort is a trap. Comfort is a great hindrance. Most people desire to live in comfort but do not want to work to earn that comfort. They would rather sleep than work hard. These people have only the present, but no future. The one who labors diligently has the present and the future because, through hard work, he has acquired certain skills necessary for managing various aspects of life.

Living in ease and comfort like a white man is a curse. I'm used to working like a black man, that's why I don't sleep much. As a result, I am who I am. People from all over the world come to learn from me because I "Plow like a black man". While others choose to relax, I choose to work hard, that is why I will always have something to contribute. Others live only to satisfy their immediate desire.

Who is better: Indigenes or Foreigners?

The research center of the portal "Job mail.ru" conducted a survey among residents of Russia. More than a third of respondents (37%) agreed that foreign specialists who came to Russia are much more diligent, and 29% consider them more purposeful and active. Among the migrants themselves, 39% consider themselves to be more purposeful than Russian citizens, which in their opinion, will further affect their advancement of the career ladder.

This study confirms our arguments about the future of plowmen, who take up the work that others do not want to do. As a result, 41% of migrant respondents replied that their originally planned goals had already been achieved, so they set new and higher goals for themselves.

Likewise, Mila Golovchenko, the head of the press service of the Internet portal for job search notes that employers are more eager to see migrants in their staff because, they are more disciplined, hard-working and less likely to work in a drunken state [65]. Doctor of Historical Sciences, Professor of Archeology and Ethnography Tatyana Titova stated; *"employers have noticed that foreigners have a more responsible attitude towards their tasks[66]"*. A similar phenomenon occurs in other countries. In particular, The Daily Mail newspaper writes that British firms also want to hire more migrants, since they are more industrious, reliable and often more qualified.

As indicated above, the "working as a Negro" approach develops the necessary skills and qualities that will always be appreciated. Please note that the work of such people is recognized. Eventually, they will turn into the engine of progress and determine the further development of the society.

The results of Mosgorstat (a statistical organization based in Moscow) research on the composition of Moscow's large and medium-sized enterprises showed that only 60% of all Russian citizens in Moscow are Muscovites. At the same time, the head of the research center of the Moscow

Psychological and Social University, Olga Vorobyeva, notes that large and medium-sized enterprises account for only 45% of jobs in Moscow. The 55% is comprised primarily of small business trade and services and is predominantly owned by foreigners.

This goes on to confirm that foreigners are not idlers; they are industrious and diligent. At the same time, people who already have enough to eat, rest on their achievements and sometimes stop working hard.

It is interesting that about 50% of those working in hospitals in Moscow are medical personnel from other towns. Another area where the expertise of visitors is in high demand is real estate business. Real estate is a very tough and demanding business. Unfortunately, company directors note that majority of Muscovite's is accustomed to sit on a salary and receive money, regardless of whether they work or not. In addition, a large percentage of women in real estate have their own apartments and a husband that is able to cater to their financial needs. Therefore, the incentives to "plow like a Negro" are much less.

Approximately 9% of visitors, according to Rosstat, are hired by banks and insurance companies. Although the majority is still employed in low positions, experts explain that provincials are quicker to make their way up and occupy the positions of department heads[67].

Therefore, we can conclude that "plowing like a Negro" is actually the way to success. If other vital qualities are added to this type of diligent labor, we can be guaranteed that such a person will be very wealthy and successful;

Migrating for Job Opportunities

In the previous examples, as we compared the work ethics of the indigenes and foreigners, we could still trace the effect of monoculturalism. If the society is monocultural, these effects can even be felt within the society.

A Russian resident- Ms. Valentine relates her story: "I am Russian, but it's appalling to hear people asking "Why did you come to Moscow?" It's almost as if they assume that the people of other provinces are undeserving of the good salaries that are available in Moscow. This is snobbery."

Snobbery is an accentuated pride of belonging to a certain formally or informally defined circle of society which is perceived as superior or elite. Those involved also jealously guard its purity, i.e. it's immiscibility with the surrounding world.

Indigenes of a country, who snob at foreigners and use offensive words like "Go back to your country" or "you don't belong here", fail to recognize that their fellow countrymen are in other countries too. If they insist that foreigners should leave their country they should also expect that their fellow countrymen in other countries would also have to leave. Is this logical?

Sometimes, we fail to put ourselves in the place of others. According to the Ministry of Labor and Social Policy, about twenty thousand Ukrainian citizens work in Africa. In addition, according to unofficial data, this number is at least five times as much[68].

Similarly, if we take the data of the institute of Demography in 2010, while 14,677 Ukrainians officially migrated to other countries, only 282 African citizens migrated to Ukraine. Out of the 282, 78 of them were Nigerian citizens[69].

If there is support for the idea of monoculture in Ukraine, then let the Ukrainians return from the USA and Canada. Let them come from all over the world. Each of them will object!

If they return, then there are fewer jobs in Ukraine, they need to be given a place to live and certain specialists will be jobless. Unfortunately, monoculture supporters aren't profound thinkers, they do not take into account global economic processes.

According to the head of the International Organization for Migration; Geoffrey Labovitsa[23] in 2007, Ukrainian labor migrants working in the EU countries alone, sent 27 billion euros to Ukraine, which is 8% of Ukrainian GDP.

People who support ideas such as "Ukraine for Ukrainians" or "Russia for Russians", have never thought thoroughly about these ideologies. Many politicians make this kind of statements out of patriotism. Since, they want to assign additional rights to the titular nation, depriving them of other inhabitants of the same country, they do not show people how faulty their proposals are. If we try to implement this scenario in reality, as I described earlier, the country will find itself in a financial and humanitarian catastrophe.

Thus, in this chapter, we were convinced that in a monocultural society, because of the exaltation of other ethnic groups, an associative division of labor along ethnic lines arises. This leads to such a DANGER as a devaluation of diligent and hard work. As a result, people become more relaxed and degraded, and foreign visitors outstrip them in the achieved results. In conclusion, I showed the absurdity of the idea that foreigners should return to their countries since the fact of having their own countrymen in other countries is not taken into account at all.

In the next chapter, I will show whether we need to borrow something from other peoples and cultures or we are «ourselves with a mustache,» and enough internal potential of the country's achievements, the existing aspects of culture.

GOLDEN TRUTH

• In the minds of most people, there is a conflict: black skin is associated with plowing, and white «European» skin - with comfort.

• The danger of monoculturalism lies in the fact that, it develops an adverse attitude towards work in which, people try to avoid hard labor and want to simply take positions of dominance over others that will carry out this work.

• If you plow and work all the time, and choose not to «live like a white man» - you have a future.

• As foreigners, this slavish-plowing is advantageous.

• In both generations, the blacks had a higher level of results on achievements in education, wage level, and employment.

• The adherent one who believes in the hard working ethics of the black man, experiences continued success and development.

• Comfort, which was not preceded by hard work, could not improve her quality of life, nor did it give her a better life, rather it worsened her condition.

• Comfort is misleading; it can cause a person to lose focus and direction in life.

• Most people desire to live in comfort but do not want to work to earn that comfort.

• Reluctance to «work like a Negro», that is to work diligently deprives a person of attaining a promising future.

• The "working as a Negro" approach develops the necessary skills and qualities that will always be appreciated.

SELF-EVALUATION TEST

1. Describe the ideal state of your profession.

a) I hold a high position, earn a lot and do nothing at all (2)

b) I lie on the beach and do nothing; my uncle from overseas sends me money every month (1)

c) I persistently and continuously progress and have a corresponding worthy financial reward (3).

2. What will you do if you win a million dollars?

A) I will continue to develop my skills and abilities; I will use money with wisdom (3)

B) I will invest money in different projects and forget about work forever (2)

C) I will buy what I have always dreamed of and enjoy life (1).

3. Assess your current behavior in the sphere of career development.

a) I work hard in spite of my income level (3)

b) I am satisfied with the current situation, so I just use it (1)

c) I strive to work hard because at the moment I can barely make ends meet (2).

4. What future would you wish for your children?

a) I want them to live like white people, give them everything that I did not have, and provide for them (1)

b) I want them to understand the value and advantage of hard work, so I will educate them so that they work hard in their professional sphere (3)

c) I want them to have a good education and a stable job (2).

RESULTS

Less than 8 points. Unfortunately, you have a wrong perception of work. You seek comfort and, most likely, do not even know about its disastrous effect. This approach can be called the desire to «live as a white man.» Thus, you devalue diligence, hard work, and progress.

8-11 points. You are characterized by a certain amount of zeal. Nevertheless, your efforts today show the desire to escape from the need to work hard. I encourage you not to run away from hard work, it is this labor that is the best investment in your life. You should reconsider your priorities and understand the influence of comfort on a person's life.

12 points. Congratulations! You have the right attitude towards work. You can call your approach in life «plow as a Negro.» Thus, you break the danger of depreciation of labor, which occurs in monocultural societies. You are building a long-term platform for your success, as you continuously develop. Take time to share and impart your value for hard work, because this attitude is beneficial not only for you but also for your family, relatives and the society at large.

RECOMMENDATIONS ON HOW TO WORK ON PRACTICAL TASKS

PLEASE NOTE: These tasks are not intended to be read-only. In order for you to make the necessary changes, you need to work through them, which is why the word «practical» appears in the title of this section of the book. Often we do this kind of exercises for marks. However, now you are doing these tasks for your own personal development. Therefore, I ask you to take the tasks seriously, because you are not doing it for the author of the book, but for you.

To get the maximum result from these tasks, it is recommended to:

1. Perform these tasks within the first 24 hours. If you delay it is more likely that you will not accomplish the tasks.

2. Study practical tasks in silence and in a calming environment. Find a quiet place where no one can disturb you: perhaps it will be a time when no one is at home or at night when everyone is asleep.

3. Make sure to reflect on the previous chapter and all the points that you have highlighted for yourself. Recall the decisions you made and write down your follow-up actions.

4. Do not forget to schedule specific time frames and determine the boundaries that you will impose on yourself. This will help you to avoid procrastination on the planned steps to change your life in a long run.

5. Find someone you can be accountable to for your decisions, or a partner to work with.

PRACTICAL TASKS

1. What do phrases like «plow as a Negro» and «live like a white man» mean to you?

2. What is the advantage of «plowing like a Negro»?

3. Why do people inevitably lose lottery wins?

4. What will happen if all the «black» work in the country will be performed by foreigners?

CHAPTER 7
THE REWARDS OF
EMBRACING OTHER
CULTURES

CHAPTER 7
THE REWARDS OF EMBRACING OTHER CULTURES

"A multicultural society does not reject the culture of the other but is prepared to listen, to see, to dialogue and, in the final analysis, to possibly accept the other's culture without compromising its own".

- Reuven Rivlin, Israeli-politician

In the previous chapter, we examined how a monocultural society influences attitudes towards work and the irreparable damage that it inflicts on the values of labor.

In this chapter, we will examine the benefits of adopting the positive attributes of other cultures and societies. Before we begin our discussion, we should look at the danger of Xenophobia which is typical for the MONOCULTURAL society.

Xenophobia is a fear or a hatred of someone or something foreign, unfamiliar or strange; the perception of a stranger as incomprehensible and perplexing, thereby leading to hostility and violence. In a monocultural society because of this arrogant and thoughtless attitude they fail to recognize the value of other people. Thus, they rob and deprive themselves of wise principles and methods that they could have learned from others.

THE KEY TO JAPAN'S ECONOMIC MIRACLE

Japan today is a highly developed country. It ranks third in the world in terms of GDP, the fourth - in terms of exports and the sixth - in terms of imports. This is one of the most technologically advanced and industrialized countries on the Earth. Looking at Tokyo's skyscrapers, it's hard to believe that 150-170 years ago Japan was ruled by samurai. How did the Japanese manage to modernize their economy much faster than their neighbors?

Earlier Japan was famous for its low-quality product. Now the word Japan is equated with quality. Policies and strategies were set forth carefully by the policy-making authorities to protect and sustain growth. Japanese firms become more flexible to go through a change process. Technological improvements in Japan contributed greatly to its economic growth because improvements of technologies in one industry influenced the growth of many other industries.

The key to Japans economic miracle is Iitoko Dori - the Japanese art of borrowing elements of other cultures and adapting them to their daily lives. American historian and philosopher of Japanese descent, Hajime Nakamura, elaborated on the admirable ability of the Japanese people not only to accept cultures from other countries but also developed the habit of adopting the most useful borrowings from other countries. However, everything that is accepted by the West, is certainly adjusted to their customs.

For Japan, the era of modernization began in 1854. After 14 years, in need of a durable lightweight industry, Japan decided to adopt the French technology. In 1873 a new textile factory was opened in the city of Tomioka, which was literally brought from France (from the machinery tools to bricks, tables, and chairs). The higher positions were occupied by the French while the Japanese workers followed their instructions and watched them closely.

Tomioka factory produced good silk but for the sake of justice, it should be noted that the production did not immediately become profitable. In fact, in 1875, the company's budget deficit amounted to 220 thousand yen. Nevertheless, in 1910 the Japanese managed to outperform the «teachers» and the factory began to produce first-class silk and export it abroad.

Iitoko Dori is one of the explanations of how the Japanese raised the economy from the post-war ruins.

Many economists point out the fact that developing countries can be modernized by attracting and assimilating technologies from more developed countries, as Japan did on a large scale in the recent past. In general, Asian countries for example, Korea, Taiwan, and Singapore have successfully modernized this way.

Author Lee Kuan Yew wrote about the Prime Minister of Singapore, who raised his country from the third world to the first. He said "I benefited from the lessons for which others paid ... I preferred to climb up, leaning on the shoulders of those who walked ahead".

In multicultural societies, there is a mutual enrichment of the cultures and the interpenetration of certain cultural elements in the course of interaction. Sometimes, what we perceive as a traditional nation is the result of a centuries-old mutual influence of different cultures. We are talking about diffusion, which has an active influence on the dynamics of culture.

Culturally, diffusion is the mutual penetration of specific cultural phenomena. According to the definition of W. Haviland [70], diffusion is the borrowing of certain cultural elements from one community to another community. Thus, thanks to the historical, natural and other processes of interaction, the infiltration and spread of cultural innovations occur. Channels of cultural diffusion are migration, tourism and other intercultural contacts in the political, social, cultural, and professional spheres.

«SO YOUR DAUGHTER MARRIED A NEGRO!"

There is a so-called Bogardus social distance scale which empirically measures people's willingness to participate in social contacts of varying degrees of closeness with members of diverse social groups, such as racial and ethnic groups. The scale asks people the extent to which they would be accepting of each:

1. Acceptance as close relatives through marriage.

2. Acceptance as personal friends.

3. Acceptance as neighbors living on the same street.

4. Acceptance as colleagues in the same profession.

5. Acceptance as citizens of my country.

6. Acceptance only as tourists in my country.

7. Would prefer not to see them in my country.

People of a monocultural society are more hostile to the idea of family reunification with an individual of another group. In such societies, people do not want their daughters to marry black men in particular.

Now, I want us to examine the characteristics of African husbands and discover how superficial this prejudice is. Let's look at the specifics of the African culture. After all, this culture is one in which men are brought up to be good husbands. So it's a mistake to think that Africans are not good husbands.

1. Defenders: The instinct to protect the people close to him is the core of his nature as a man. He is a man and he has pride, he is the lion of his family; strong and protective. He guards his wife and children, as a bodyguard protects important people. He has the attitude of a special unit force, which has been entrusted with the greatest jewelry. As soon as something poses a threat to his family, it immediately becomes his personal threat which he must neutralize.

2. Providers: In the African family, from childhood, boys are raised with the understanding and the teaching that the key role of a man is to provide for his family. Moreover, he is taught that he is the provider of not only his immediate family but also his extended family: parents, brothers, sisters, nephews and various close family members. He inherently cares for his parents and even grandmothers, grandfathers - he seeks a good relationship with them. The same applies to the parents of the wife. His reputation is dependent on the quality of help he provides to his closest relatives.

If you marry an African, you will marry a man who takes his responsibility for the family very seriously. Even if circumstances sometimes are against him, he will never stop trying to fulfill his role as the head of the family. All the decisions that he makes will be weighed in terms of influence not only on himself but also on his wife and the entire family.

3. Value for marriage: Marriage is a sign of maturity for an African man. It is having a family, in his perception as well as in the perception of others, that transitions him from boyhood to manhood. Therefore, he takes this step very seriously. His wife and family are now building up his identity. As a result, he is inclined to be dedicated to his family. MY wife, MY children are words that he proudly highlights. He will take his wife to his acquaintances and praise her with the most subtle compliments.

An African who runs his house well is automatically a story of success in his society. In fact, how strong and happy his family is, determines the basic level of his success. However, the man who dishonors his wife is disrespected and ridiculed in his society.

Marriage for an African is more than just a relationship. It is a bearing wall in the structure of his life. He sees all his plans through the prism of the family. There is a common belief that a wife and a child always come with a blessing. And no African will miss out on the opportunity to receive a blessing. That's why he values his family so much!

The American research organization, Pew Research Center conducted a global study, in which it sought out people's opinions on divorce. In total, over 40,000 respondents in 40 countries were interviewed. On average

in 40 countries, 24% of respondents had a negative opinion about divorce, while the interregional differences are quite large. 60-80% Africans that participated in the survey responded that divorce is morally unacceptable. In the EU countries, on the contrary, a very small percentage of the population considers divorce to be immoral. In Spain, France, Germany, Great Britain, Canada, Australia, the proportion of those who think divorce is morally unacceptable is less than 10%. In Russia, the percentage disapproving of divorce was 22%, the same as in Poland and the United States.

Directly, the level of divorce in African countries is much less than in Europe, the United States, Canada, etc.[71][73] and, according to the population census in the United States, 15% of all marriages are between people of different races. Amazingly, the divorce rate among mixed marriages is lower than the overall level of divorce in the US. The lowest rate being in families where one person represents a white race and the second is an African American[74].

Naturally, people in each country have their own weaknesses. For example, among some groups of Africans polygamy is permissible. Although educated, Christian Africans refuse such a pseudo-culture, it is still worthwhile to analyze soberly and judiciously every single case.

4. Easily satisfied: The proverb "the way to the heart of a man is through the stomach" has African roots. Prepare his favorite national food - that is all he needs to be happy. He also likes to dress well and appreciates a clean house. We can say that he is not picky.

5. Loves adventures: The African is not averse to plunging into something new for him. He will be open to learning about other cultures and adopting a new one from his wife. Therefore, some things that at the beginning of marriage were alien to him, he can acquire in the process.

6. An Extended family: African have large families. African families are quite close to each other. The wife will be part of a larger community which supports one another. She will have relatives all around the world and their children will be able to visit them. The children will have the opportunity to learn a new language and culture. If a woman is married to a foreigner, it is likely that the children will at least know an additional language.

7. They show noble behavior: This may not be expressed by the man opening the door or helping the lady to remove her coat. The romanticism of Europe is foreign to them. Although if the man studied abroad, he may show gentlemanliness in this way. They indeed have good manners and a sense of chivalrous prowess which is inherent in Africans. Although they come from countries where women's rights are not at the highest level, but it is there that women are most cared for. Therefore, be assured that inside of him the potential of a gallant, courteous gentleman is laid.

8. Industrious: They have an amazing enthusiasm that motivates them to pay any price to achieve prosperity. Therefore, this attitude will be the atmosphere of the family - dedicated to creating a better future for themselves and their families. They are extremely hardworking.

9. Self-Sufficient: Due to the fact that in many African countries there is poverty and civil wars, Africans appreciate the stability and comfort that they are able to acquire in life, in particular, the comfort that comes with having a wife. Unlike the spoiled local residents who are accustomed to a certain, comfortable way of life, the African man will not take anything for granted, because life has helped him set the right priorities.

Since he had to leave his home, it means he can cook and take care of himself. That is why when someone comes along to help him with this, he is greatly appreciative. He values being taken care of, he doesn't perceive it as being dependent, needy or pitiful.

10. Neat: A majority of Africans are exceptionally hygienic, well-dressed and elegant. Perhaps once again this is due to the fact they do not take what they have for granted.

Thus, we are convinced that the prejudices inherent in individuals of many monocultural societies in relation to black husbands are devoid of logic. On the contrary, we find that foreigners can be even more enviable husbands, wives, and relatives in general, compared to the natives of the local population.

Despite the virtue and quality of African families, I would still advise Europeans or people from other cultures not to hurry to marry an African or another foreigner. It is necessary to visit the country, learn the culture and decide where the family will live. If a man lives in a foreign country, he must, first of all, understand the culture, the expectation of his wife and know how to please her.

Many marry blindly claiming: «We fell in love ...» Falling in love - is one thing, but it is essential to study the specifics of culture. When emotions pass, then all there will be is, reality, in particular, the reality of cultural differences. I know that there are successful interracial and intercultural marriages, but this success is a result of hard work. Imagine, if people of the same culture cannot get along, then it would prove even more difficult for individuals of different races. There is a need for preparation and determination to work on our marriage.

Lessons from other cultures

We need to develop an attitude of tolerance towards other nations and cultures. According to the Philosophical Encyclopedic Dictionary, tolerance is defined as acceptance and open-mindedness to different kind of views, customs, and habits.

The very term «tolerance» is of medical origin. It denotes the complete or partial absence of an immunological reaction; That is, the loss or decrease (in a living organism) of the ability to produce antibodies. In the interethnic, intercultural context, we tend to develop unique antibodies: this is our defensive reaction to a foreign body that enters our environment. The more monocultural a society is, the more unreceptive and intolerant it is in respect to people that are different.

We label and mark everything unfamiliar as – "strange", "enemy", "unknown", "fearful".

Skip Ross in his book "Say yes to your potential" mentions such a case. We took about thirty children to a hill next to a launch off site and lined them up so that they could make an exciting descent down the hill. They believed that the sledding in summer was a real adventure. However, I noticed that one little boy, quietly left the line when it was his turn and stood at the very end. He did this several times. «Now it's your turn, Kenny, go ahead!» I told him. «You know, Mr. Ross, I don't think I will go this time, maybe I will go some other time.» «Kenny, everyone is having a great time. Come on, you'll like it. « «No, Mr. Ross, I think I would rather go down on foot.» «I'm sorry, Kenny, but that's not the way. It's too steep a descent. But he refused, so I forced him to be seated and sat down myself from behind, holding him with his legs and hands, we were pushed down. Kenny squealed: he screamed «No, no, stop, help!» for about twenty meters until we made a turn. At that point, his words changed to «A-ah-ah-ah-ah-ah-ah-ah!» as we dashed downhill. At the end of our ride, Kenny jumped out of the sleigh, grabbed my arm and shouted: «Mr. Ross, let's go one more time!

Similarly, each of us has a process of getting to know the unknown; initially it may be strange even frightening, but eventually, it becomes desirable and exciting! Ignorance and a lack of experience have created the ground for a harsh non-acceptance of everything else. A closer association with the things we assume to be strange can lead to the development of tolerance, and the "antibodies" of our monocultural teaching will lose the incentives to originate. However, let's take a trip to the diverse and multicultural planet Earth at least on the pages of this book.

In Hong Kong, a native of the USSR passed by a café and saw a lot of flowers. He supposed that perhaps someone had died. However, it turned out quite differently; these people came to celebrate the opening of the café and to congratulate the owner. Isn't it wonderful?

While among the Slavs the prevalent attitude is depicted in this proverb: «It does not matter that my hut has burned down. The main thing is that the neighbor's cow also died" Another example of this attitude is illustrated in this anecdote: «God asked the peasant what he would like, the peasant replied: «I do not need anything; I just want my neighbor's house to burn down.» Therefore, we can learn from other cultures how to not be jealous, but to rejoice at the success of other people!

Chuvashia is a republic within the Russian Federation. Since ancient times the Chuvash people have believed that the most terrible curse is the curse of a mother, which will come true. The Chuvash people greatly honor and esteem their mothers.

In Chuvash families, women have never been thought of as less significant, equality has always been the case, and there have never been customs of degrading women. Spouses respected each other, and therefore divorce was rare in Chuvash families. The elders of the Chuvash community have a saying concerning married couples: «The woman is a deity in the house and the man is the king in the house.»

The Chuvash people had strong families. Couples treated each other with devotion, loyalty, respect. In some traditions, it is said that the immorality of women or men was a disgrace. If a man was accused of immorality, he was brought to justice before the court of the community and evicted from the village. The father always played a significant role in the upbringing of children.

Is this not an example for today's Slavic people? Children ought not to humiliate, insult, nor beat their mothers, but emulate how the Chuvash people treated them with such reverence and honor.

Canada. If you obtain a discount card from a certain store then you acquire a lifetime guarantee for your purchased good. Of course, I am sure you are thinking that this is nonsense; you are analyzing how this will be used by all kinds of crooks. Yes, there are crooks, but they are few. Obviously, you will not bring a worn out dress for a refund or return a ten-year-old TV. You will be looked upon as a madman. However, you know that whenever your TV genuinely breaks down, it will either be repaired or replaced. The store does for it because it values you.

Furthermore, if the season of sales is beginning the following day, they will send you an e-mail, so that you can come two hours ahead of the official start of the sales. This means you can buy everything you need without queuing and without the large crowds.

We have littered gullies in many cities. Sometimes they are quite large when the authorities do not know what to do with the gullies, they turn into a garbage dump. In Canada, they do things differently: they create micro-parks in every gully. They plant grass and trees and set benches in the gullies, thereby creating a beautiful environment

Our fellow countrymen had the following experience: they were driving by car in an absolutely remote place. All around was a virgin forest, about 150 kilometers in both directions there were no housings. Suddenly they saw a garbage truck, which was moving slowly in front of them. The driver was sitting at the wheel, and the second worker was standing at the back, at the open garbage can. The worker carefully looked around. Suddenly the truck braked, the worker jumped off and walked ten meters into the forest. Then he immediately returned, with a paper cup on a long stick, someone had thrown it out of their car. You see, there is not a single person in this forest, but, apparently, this cup in the forest is an offense to the Canadian.

Singapore. The government allocates 20% of its budget for the development of the education sector! It is a nation that is obsessed with self-development. Openly in bookstores and libraries around the country, you will meet people of all ages from young children to old people who sit right on the floor and just read books. You can meet an ordinary 7-year-old boy in the subway, who is reading a book about family values. As a result, they have managed to build one of the world's best education systems, which has trained the very specialists who brought the country to the highest level: the gross national product per capita is one of the highest in the world.

There are significant advantages to traveling to other countries. This experience brings an expansion of consciousness. If you visit other nations and cultures, you can achieve educational and worldview improvements in a significant way. This is an opportunity to learn about other views, methodologies, and accomplishments.

Scientists have long established that changing environment helps to eliminate depression and, as a result, improves health. You will be surprised but previously if a person had the following symptom they were treated with a round-the-world trip:

- Depression

- Apathy

- Changes in appetite and weight

- Insomnia

- Drowsiness

- Lethargy

- Decreased efficiency

Arriving in an unfamiliar place helps you to cope with the manifestation of depression because you will be distracted from the ordinary home environment. New acquaintances and interaction with interesting people influence the emergence of positive emotions. Moreover, regular trips give a person a sense of happiness and improve mood. This improves the quality of life.

Due to the experience of being in new places our horizons and knowledge of foreign languages expand, which also influences the development and mental health of the person.

So, in this chapter, we have considered the advantage of being open to other peoples and cultures, in order to be able to adopt the good that they have: customs, approaches, principles, technologies. It became obvious that people from other nations and cultures may turn out to be good relatives. Noteworthy was the fact that it influenced the development of Japan as a highly developed country in its art to adopt the necessary elements from other cultures and adapt to its conditions. Therefore, the benefits of interaction between different cultures translate into additional knowledge, incentives and ways to achieve global and individual goals.

GOLDEN TRUTH

• The key to Japans economic miracle is Iitoko Dori - the Japanese art of borrowing elements of other cultures and adapting them to their daily lives.

• I benefited from the lessons for which others paid ... I preferred to climb up, leaning on the shoulders of those who walked ahead" Lee Kuan Yew.

• In multicultural societies, there is a mutual enrichment of the cultures and the interpenetration of certain cultural elements in the course of interaction.

• People of a monocultural society are more hostile to the idea of family reunification with an individual of another group.

• We find that foreigners can be even more enviable husbands, wives, and relatives in general, compared to the natives of the local population.

• Due to the experience of being in new places our horizons and knowledge of foreign languages expand, which also influences the development and mental health of the person

SELF-EVALUATION TEST

1. What will your attitude be if there is a teacher in your society, an expert in a sphere that is important to you, but from an entirely different ethnic group?

A) Why did he come here, aren't our teachers capable enough? Let him go to his homeland! (1)

B) I will learn from him the professional skills and knowledge that he possesses (3)

C) It will be normal, but I will personally ignore him(2).

2. How will you react if you have a colleague or a neighbor of a different culture?

A) I will impose our culture on him, after all, he is the one that came here(1)

B) I will learn about the richness of his culture (3)

C) We will just work together, live in the neighborhood but I will keep myself separate from him (2).

3. What will you do if in your professional sphere you do not find a solution to a problem?

A) I'll turn to friends, colleagues for advice (1)

B) I will look for how this problem was addressed in other organizations in my country/region (2)

C) Together with the two previous items, I will begin to study foreign experience and adapt it to local conditions (3).

4. Imagine that your organization has decided to fully pay for your vacation. Where will you go?

A) I'll go to the dacha, buy a lot of food and «depart» from work (1)

B) I will go to a resort in my country or even in another - and I will visit all the possible places of entertainment (2)

C) I will fly to another country to get acquainted with another culture and learn about unique positive methods and techniques (3).

RESULTS

Less than 8 points. Sadly, you limit yourself to most of the opportunities that life has prepared for you. The world was preparing for your arrival, preparing in different regions and cultures. But you cut yourself off from this vast amount of riches that are contained in other ethnicities, etc.. The root of this attitude is pride and ignorance. You need to honestly analyze how the things you use in everyday life, in your profession, have been influenced by people of other nations.

8-11 points. You are fairly neutral about having people from other groups in your community. Although at the same time, you ignore their presence and, accordingly, deprive yourself of virtues that could enrich your life. You are not initiative enough to passionately study and adopt those positive approaches that give others result. You should go to the next level and become active in your interaction with people of other groups and races.

12 points. Congratulations! You are an extremely open person and are humble enough to learn from others. People from other cultural and social groups can feel comfortable with you because you show genuine interest. You can safely say that, because you have discovered the access to the abyss of the advantages of other countries and peoples you will avoid some unnecessary situations in life.

RECOMMENDATIONS ON HOW TO WORK ON PRACTICAL TASKS

PLEASE NOTE: These tasks are not intended to be read-only. In order for you to make the necessary changes, you need to work through them, which is why the word «practical» appears in the title of this section of the book. Often we do this kind of exercises for marks. However, now you are doing these tasks for your own personal development. Therefore, I ask you to take the tasks seriously, because you are not doing it for the author of the book, but for you.

To get the maximum result from these tasks, it is recommended to:

1. Perform these tasks within the first 24 hours. If you delay it is more likely that you will not accomplish the tasks.

2. Study practical tasks in silence and in a calming environment. Find a quiet place where no one can disturb you: perhaps it will be a time when no one is at home or at night when everyone is asleep.

3. Make sure to reflect on the previous chapter and all the points that you have highlighted for yourself. Recall the decisions you made and write down your follow-up actions.

4. Do not forget to schedule specific time frames and determine the boundaries that you will impose on yourself. This will help you to avoid procrastination on the planned steps to change your life in a long run.

5. Find someone you can be accountable to for your decisions, or a partner to work with.

PRACTICAL TASKS

1. What prevents us from applying positive experience and knowledge from other ethnic, social, etc. Groups?

2. What are the benefits of interacting with other ethnic, social, cultural groups?

3. Name at least 5 advantages of studying foreign languages

Conclusion

So our journey has come to an end along the back streets of a monocultural society. We were convinced of how DANGEROUS to remain a MONOCULTURE IN THE XXI CENTURY!

According to a study conducted by the National Policy Institute, by 2060 the number of white people will drop to 10%. While in 1950 in the world population of white people were 28%, and Africans were three times less - 9%. The situation will change in a diametrical way - people of African descent will be about 25% in 2060, and of European origin - 9.8% 75.

In the United States, according to the forecast of the Census Bureau, by 2060 the proportion of whites among Americans will drop to 43%. Thus, this group will become the only race whose number will decrease in the next half century.

The general distribution of the world population will be as follows: 29% - people from Central Asia; 25% came from Africa; 17% from East Asia; 9.8% from Europe; 8% from Southeast Asia; 7% from Arab countries; 4% - other ethnic groups.

Therefore, every society will face the challenge to create harmonious conditions for a multicultural interaction.

At the moment, the process of globalization of the economic, political and cultural spheres of life becomes all-embracing. As a result, migration of capital, labor, economic and technological processes throughout the planet, as well as the rapprochement of cultures of different countries, is becoming a result.

Therefore, if any country does not rebuild now and does not cease to be a monocultural society, it inevitably awaits a catastrophe.

If we sum up the dangers of monoculture, then we will have powerful arguments to take active steps to change the current state of things:

1. The desire to isolate people who are not like them

2. The unquenchable nature of hatred of difference, the growing intolerance of an increasing number of groups of people

3. Crimes against humanity

4. Repression of logic and obvious facts

5. Stereotyped and stigmatized thinking

6. An attitude based on conjecture

7. Restriction of the worldview, deprivation of the ability to discover truth and justice

8. Creating the ground for future conflicts

9. Inability to adequately assess their position, misconception about their own shortcomings and the advantages of others

10. Division of people by intellect, social groups, classes and achievements

11. Unreasonable pride and arrogance

12. Intellectual Fascism

13. Relationships based on material wealth

14. Satisfaction with your own advantages and ignoring the needs of others

15. Wars, revolutions, and bloodshed

16. Judgments about people on the basis of their appearance

17. Development of subconscious racism

18. Lack of objectivity in judgments and opposite judgments based on the people's belonging to their own group

19. The basis of self-assessment solely on belonging to a monocultural society

20. Acceptance of the initial limited information about other people and the resulting distorted interpretation of the external attributes of people

21. Negative impact on mental, physical health and effectiveness of people who experience prejudice

22. Attitudes toward work, in which people seek to avoid hard work, and want to simply take over the positions of domination over others that will carry out this work

23. The state of relaxation and degradation, ahead of foreign visitors in the results achieved

24. Stealing yourself, depriving those wise principles and approaches that others have.

The lack of a civic position in society against the infringement of the rights of racial, ethnic, national, cultural minorities - leads to aggravation of the problem and to huge irreversible negative consequences, losses. So I can not be silent, and I wrote this book. I believe that the proposed arguments will help prevent a repeat of the mistakes of history on a large scale.

Sunday Adelaja

REFERENCE

1. Stephan H. Astourian. Genocidal Process: Reflections on the Armeno-Turkish Polarization // Hovannisian. The Armenian genocide: history, politics, ethics. — P. 68—69.

2. Totten, Bartrop, Jacobs. Dictionary of Genocide. — P. 19.

3. Crime, security in SA. Lee Rondganger.

4. Italian Rwanda convict flown home. BBC – Электронный ресурс: http://news.bbc.co.uk/2/hi/africa/7268739.stm.

5. Коллет Брейкман. Подстрекательство в геноциду – Электронный ресурс. – http://www.africana.ru/news/pain/war/Tutsi/brakeman.htm.

6. American Jewish Committee, Harry Schneiderman and Julius B. Maller, eds., American Jewish Year Book, Vol. 48 (1946—1947), Press of Jewish Publication Society of America, Philadelphia, 1946, page 599.

7. Бессонов Н.В. Цыганская трагедия. 1941-1945. Факты, документы, воспоминания. Том 2: Вооруженный отпор. СПб. - 2010г.

8. Нюрнбергский процесс. Преступления против человечности (том 5).

9. Замечания и предложения «Восточного министерства» по генеральному плану «Ост»/ Научно-просветительский журнал «Скепсис».

10. Hans J. Massaquoi Destined to Witness: Growing Up Black in Nazi Germany. — Harper Perennial, 2001.

11. Герлант У. Эвтаназия — преступление национал-социалистов // Вестник Ассоциации психиатров Украины. — 2013. — № 2.

12. Rose, Rick. «Museum of Pain». The Advocate, October 19, 1993.

13. Соціальна робота: [в 3-х ч.] / [за ред. Т. Семигіної, І. Григи]; Нац. ун-т. «Києво-Могилянська академія». Школа соціальної роботи ім. В. І. Полтавця. – К.: Видавничий дім «Києво-Могилянська академія», 2004.

14. Яковенко В.С. Ребёнок-сирота: развитие, воспитание, усыновление. – Кировоград, 1997.

15. Рич Н. Социальная работа с детьми в США. Личные размышления // Социальная работа в Украине: теория и практика. – 2002.

16. Картинг П.Д. Возвращение в сообщество. – К.: Сфера, 2001.

17. М. Кордуэлл. психология от А до Я: Словарь-справочник, 2000 г.

18. И.Гофман. Стигма: Заметки об управлении испорченной идентичностью.

19. Урология: учебник. Под редакцией Д.Ю. Пушкаря.

20. Kearney P., Whelton M., Reynolds K., et al. Worldwide prevalence of hypertension: a systematic review. //J. of Hypertens. -2004. -Vol.22. -P.11-19.

21. Website- http://www.gks.ru/bgd/regl/b12_11/IssWWW.exe/Stg/d1/02-07.htm.

22. Website-http://news.finance.ua/ru/news/~/302921.

23. Website-http://rus.newsru.ua finance /22mar 2008/zarob.html.

24. Website-http://www.gazeta.ru/news/business /2011/05/12/n_1834985.shtml.

25. Website-http://www.vestifinance.ruarticles/28909.

26. Website-http://rodovid.me/saharin/v-mireezhegodno-30-produktov-vybrasyvaetsya-na-svalku.html.

27. Любушин Н.П. Экономический анализ. 3-е изд., перераб. и доп. - М.: . - 575 с. , 2010.

28. «Report for Selected Countries and Subjects (PPP valuation of country GDP)». IMF. October 2014.

29. Data (2014-12-16). «»Gross domestic product 2013, PPP», World Bank, accessed on 18 December 2014». Data.worldbank.org. Retrieved 2014-12-18.

30. World Economic Outlook Database, October 2014.

31. «GDP (current US$)». World Development Indicators. World Bank. Retrieved 18 December 2014.

32. The Fastest Billion – the story behind Africa' s Economic Revolution: http://africanbusinessmagazine.com/profiles-and-interviews/profile/why-africa-will-rule-the-21st-century/#sthash.r0FxjvWu.dpuf.

33. Encyclopedic Dictionary, 2009.

34. Website-http://trace.tennessee.edu/utk_chanhonoproj.

35. An Economic History of Africa by Peter Wickins.

36. Africa since 1800 by Roland Oliver & Anthony Atmore.

37. Understanding conflict and war: Vol. 4: war, power, peace. Chapter 16. Causes And Conditions Of International Conflict And War. By R.J. Rummel.

38. Angela Davis, Women, Race and Class (1981).

39. For Gypsies, Eugenics is a Modern Problem — Czech Practice Dates to Soviet Era, Newsdesk, 2006.

40. Website- http://www.kommersant.ru/doc/13746.

41. Herrnstein, R., & Murray, C. (1994). The bell curve. New York: Free Press.

42. Мифы о генетическом предопределении IQ, Фридман В., Фридман М. – Электронный ресурс: http://www.elektron2000.com/fridman_Vlad_Mar_0302.html.

43. Психология: учеб. для гуманитар. Вузов. Дружинин В Н.

44. Холодная М.А., Кострикина И.С, 2002. Особенности когнитивных стилей импульсивность/рефлективность и ригидность/гибкость познавательного контроля у лиц с высокими и сверхпороговыми значениями IQ // Психол. журн. Т. 21. № 4. С. 46-56.

45. Race, Intelligence and IQ: Are Blacks Smarter than Whites? By Bernie Douglas, 2008.

46. Raven J., 1989. The Raven Progressive Matrices: A review of national norming studies and ethnic and socio-economic variation within the United States. //J. of Educat. Measurement. V. 26. P. 1-16.

47. Logan, J.R, Deane, G (2003). Black Diversity in Metropolitan America.Lewis Mumford Center for Comparative Urban Regional Research University Albany.

48. Website-http://medvesti.com/zdorovie/dusha/795-diskriminaciya-mozhet-privesti-k-narusheniyu-psihicheskogo-zdorovya.html.

49. Williams D.R. (2005). The Health of U.S. Racial and Ethnic Populations. The Journals of Gerontology Series B: Psychological Sciences and Social Sciences 60:S53-S62 (2005)

50. The Economist (1996). 339 (7965): 27-28.

51. Arthur, John (2000). Invisible Sojourners: African Immigrant Diaspora in the United States. Prager Westport, CT.

52. Selassie, Bereket H. (1996). Washington's New African Immigrants. In Urban Odyssey: A Multicultural History of Washington D.C. Francine Cuno Cary, ed. Chapter 15 Smithsonian Institution Press.

53. Nesbitt, N.F. (2002). African Intellectuals in the Belly of the Beast: Migration, Identity and the Politics of Exile. African Issues 30: 1, 2002.

54. Charles C.Z, Massey, D.S., Mooney, M. and Kimberly C. Torres, (2007). Black Immigrants and Black Natives Attending Selective Colleges and universities in the United States. American Journal of Education 113 (Feb. 2007).

55. US Census Bureau, Census 2000. «5% Public Use Microdata Sample.»

56. Kent, M.M.(2007): Immigration and America's Black Population. Population Bulletin 62, no. 4 (2007).

57. The Journal of Blacks in Higher Education, No. 26 (Winter, 1999-2000). African Immigrants in the United States are the Nation's Most Highly Educated Group. pp. 60-61doi:10.2307/2999156.

58. Cross, T. (1994). Black Africans Now the Most Educated Group in British Society. The Journal of Blacks in Higher Education, No. 3 (spring, 1994), pp.92-93.

59. Dustmann, C, Theodoropoulos, N (2006): Ethnic Minority Immigrants and their Children in Britain. Centre for Research and Analysis of Migration, Department of Economics, University College London.

60. Dixon, D. (2006). Characteristics of the African Born in the United States. Migration Policy Institute. January, 20, 2006.

61. Li Y., Heath A. (2006) Labour market trajectories of minority ethnic groups in Britain: 1972-2005, Presentation at the UPTAP Seminar, LGA, London, 28 November.

62. Jensen, A. R. (1980). Bias in mental testing. New York: Free Press.

63. Gottfredson, L. S. (1986). Societal consequences of the g factor in employment. Journal of Vocational Behavior, 29, 379-410.

64. Herrnstein, R., & Murray, C. (1994). The bell curve. New York: Free Press.

65. Website- http://www.tv100.ru/news/migranty-bolshe-trudyatsya-i-menshe-pyut-77144.

66. Website- http://www.expertrt.ru/tema/item/317-nado-ponimat-kakie-lyudi-nam-nuzhny.html.

67. Website-http://www.kp.ru/daily/25851.4/2820283.

68. Website-http://podrobnosti.ua/podrobnosti/2008/04/28/518689.html.

69. Website-http://zn.ua/SOCIETY/zhelayuschih_poselitsya_v_ukraine_v_dva_raza_bolshe,_chem_uehat.html.

70. Haviland W.A. Cultural Anthropology. 9-th ed. USA, Orlando: Harcourt Btace College Publishers, 1999.

71. Website- http://www.edivorcepapers.com/divorce-statistics/divorce-statistics-europe.html.

72. Website - http://www.divorcemag.com/statistics/statsWorld.shtml

73. Website- http://www.divorcereform.org/gul.html.

74. Education Resources Information Center/US Department of Education.

75. Whites Down To 10% Of World Population By 2060" Does It Matter? By Patrick J. Buchanan.

SUNDAY ADELAJA'S
BIOGRAPHY

Pastor Sunday Adelaja is the Founder and Senior Pastor of The Embassy of the Blessed Kingdom of God for All Nations Church in Kyiv, Ukraine.

Sunday Adelaja is a Nigerian-born Leader, Thinker, Philosopher, Transformation Strategist, Pastor, Author and Innovator who lives in Kiev, Ukraine.

At 19, he won a scholarship to study in the former Soviet Union. He completed his master's program in Belorussia State University with distinction in journalism.

At 33, he had built the largest evangelical church in Europe — The Embassy of the Blessed Kingdom of God for All Nations.

Sunday Adelaja is one of the few individuals in our world who has been privileged to speak in the United Nations, Israeli Parliament, Japanese Parliament and the United States Senate.

The movement he pioneered has been instrumental in reshaping lives of people in the Ukraine, Russia and about 50 other nations where he has his branches.

His congregation, which consists of ninety-nine percent white Europeans, is a cross-cultural model of the church for the 21st century.

His life mission is to advance the Kingdom of God on earth by raising a generation of history makers who will live for a cause larger, bigger and greater than themselves. Those who will live like Jesus and transform every sphere of the society in every nation as a model of the Kingdom of God on earth.

His economic empowerment program has succeeded in raising over 200 millionaires in the short period of three years.

Sunday Adelaja is the author of over 300 books, many of which are translated into several languages including Russian, English, French, Chinese, German, etc.

His work has been widely reported by world media outlets such as The Washington Post, The Wall Street Journal, New York Times, Forbes, Associated Press, Reuters, CNN, BBC, German, Dutch and French national television stations.

Pastor Sunday is happily married to his "Princess" Bose Dere-Adelaja. They are blessed with three children: Perez, Zoe and Pearl.

Bill Clinton —
42Nd President Of The
United States (1993–2001),
Former Arcansas State
Governor

Ariel "Arik" Sharon —
Israeli Politician, Israeli
Prime Minister (2001–2006)

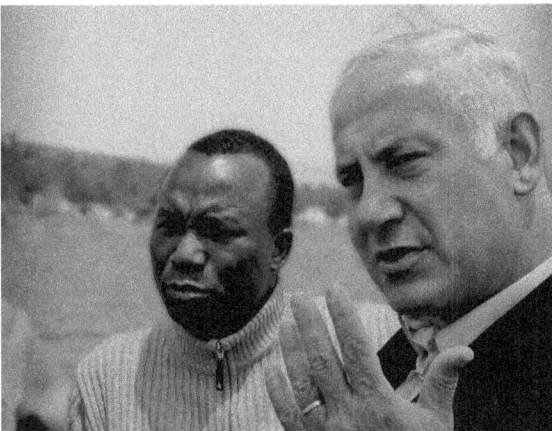

Benjamin Netanyahu —
Statesman Of Israel. Israeli
Prime Minister (1996–1999),
Acting Prime Minister
(From 2009)

Jean ChrEtien —
Canadian Politician,
20[Th] Prime Minister Of
Canada, Minister Of Justice
Of Canada, Head Of Liberan
Party Of Canada

Rudolph Giuliani —
American Political Actor,
Mayor Of New York Served
From 1994 To 2001. Actor
Of Republican Party

Colin Powell —
Is An American Statesman
And A Retired Four-Star
General In The Us Army,
65[Th] United States Secretary
Of State

Peter J. Daniels —
Is A Well-Known And
Respected Australian
Christian International
Business Statesman Of
Substance

Madeleine
Korbel Albright —
An American Politician And
Diplomat, 64[Th] United States
Secretary Of State

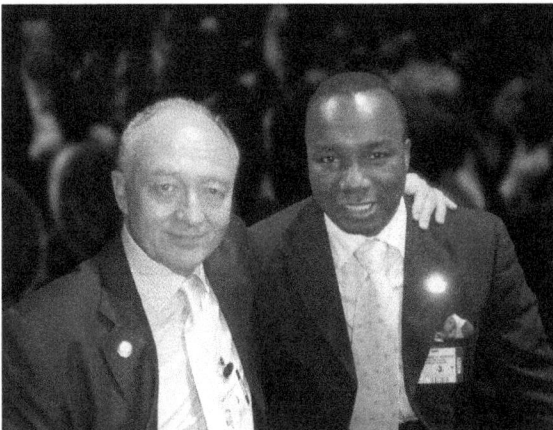

Kenneth Robert
Livingstone —
An English Politician,
1[St] Mayor Of London
(4 May 2000 – 4 May
2008), Labour Party
Representative

Sir Richard Charles Nicholas Branson — English Business Magnate, Investor And Philanthropist. He Founded The *Virgin Group,* Which Controls More Than 400 Companies

Mel Gibson — American Actor And Filmmaker

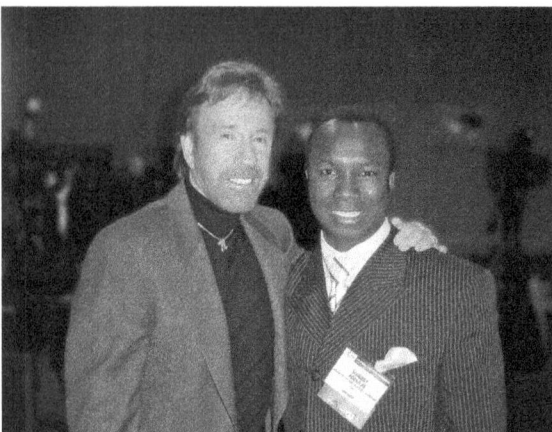

Chuck Norris — American Martial Artist, Actor, Film Producer And Screenwriter

Christopher Tucker —
American Actor
And Comedian

Bernice Albertine King —
American Minister Best
Known As The Youngest
Child Of Civil Rights Leaders
Martin Luther King Jr. And
Coretta Scott King Andrew

Andrew Young — American
Politician, Diplomat, And
Activist, 14Th United States
Ambassador To The United
Nations, 55Th Mayor Of
Atlanta

General Wesley Kanne Clark — 4-Star General And Nato Supreme Allied Commander

Dr. Sunday Adelaja's family:
Perez, Pearl, Zoe and Pastor Bose Adelaja

FOLLOW
SUNDAY ADELAJA
ON SOCIAL MEDIA

Subscribe And Read Pastor Sunday's Blog:
www.sundayadelajablog.com

**Follow these links and listen to over 200
of Pastor Sunday`s Messages free of charge:**
http://sundayadelajablog.com/content/

Follow Pastor Sunday on Twitter:
www.twitter.com/official_pastor

**Join Pastor Sunday's Facebook
page to stay in touch:**
www.facebook.com/
pastor.sunday.adelaja

**Visit our websites for more
information about Pastor
Sunday's ministry:**
http://www.godembassy.com
http://www.
pastorsunday.com
http://sundayadelaja.de

CONTACT

FOR DISTRIBUTION OR TO ORDER
BULK COPIES OF THIS BOOK,
PLEASE CONTACT US:

USA
CORNERSTONE PUBLISHING
info@thecornerstonepublishers.com
+1 (516) 547-4999
www.thecornerstonepublishers.com

AFRICA
SUNDAY ADELAJA MEDIA LTD.
E-mail: btawolana@hotmail.com
+2348187518530, +2348097721451, +2348034093699

LONDON, UK
PASTOR ABRAHAM GREAT
abrahamagreat@gmail.com
+447711399828, +441908538141

KIEV, UKRAINE
pa@godembassy.org
Mobile: +380674401958

BEST SELLING BOOKS BY DR. SUNDAY ADELAJA
AVAILABLE ON AMAZON.COM AND OKADABOOKS.COM

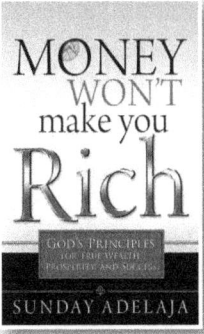

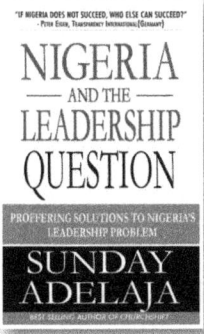

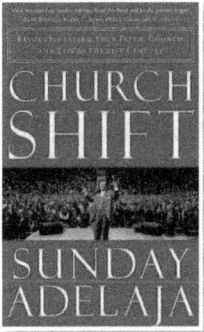

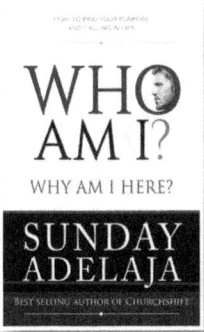

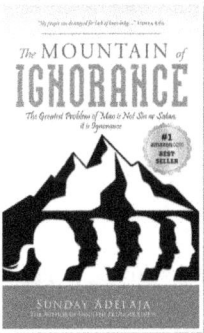

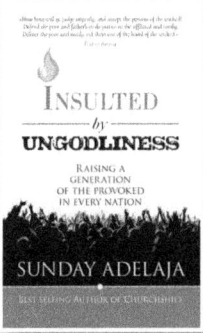

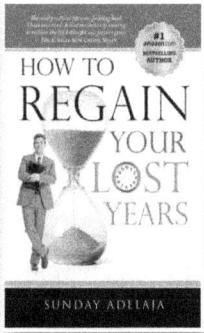

Best Selling Books by Dr. Sunday Adelaja
Available on Amazon.com and Okadabooks.com

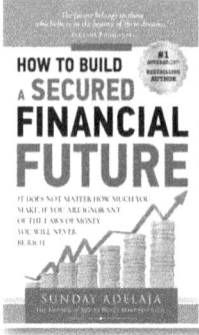

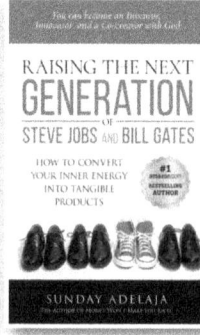

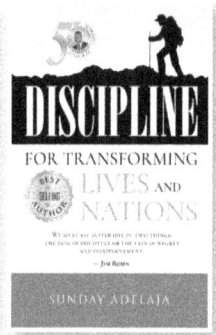

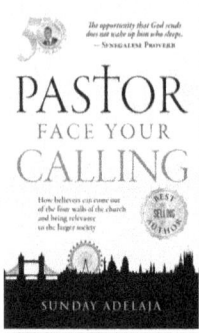

FOR DISTRIBUTION OR TO ORDER BULK COPIES OF THIS BOOKS, PLEASE CONTACT US:

USA | CORNERSTONE PUBLISHING
E-mail: info@thecornerstonepublishers.com, +1 (516) 547-4999
www.thecornerstonepublishers.com

AFRICA | SUNDAY ADELAJA MEDIA LTD.
E-mail: btawolana@hotmail.com
+2348187518530, +2348097721451, +2348034093699

LONDON, UK | PASTOR ABRAHAM GREAT
E-mail: abrahamagreat@gmail.com, +447711399828, +441908538141

KIEV, UKRAINE |
E-mail: pa@godembassy.org, Mobile: +380674401958

GOLDEN JUBILEE SERIES BOOKS
BY DR. SUNDAY ADELAJA

FOR DISTRIBUTION OR TO ORDER BULK COPIES OF THIS BOOKS, PLEASE CONTACT US:

USA | CORNERSTONE PUBLISHING
E-mail: info@thecornerstonepublishers.com, +1 (516) 547-4999
www.thecornerstonepublishers.com

AFRICA | SUNDAY ADELAJA MEDIA LTD.
E-mail: btawolana@hotmail.com
+2348187518530, +2348097721451, +2348034093699

LONDON, UK | PASTOR ABRAHAM GREAT
E-mail: abrahamagreat@gmail.com, +447711399828, +441908538141

KIEV, UKRAINE |
E-mail: pa@godembassy.org, Mobile: +380674401958

.

www.ingramcontent.com/pod-product-compliance
Lightning Source LLC
Chambersburg PA
CBHW031151270326
41931CB00006B/230